THE POWER OF THE CAT

THE POWER OF THE CAT

Ann Walker

CHIVERS

| British Library Cataloguing in Publication Data available |

This Large Print edition published by AudioGO Ltd, Bath, 2013.
Published by arrangement with the Author

U.K. Hardcover   ISBN   978 1 4713 3541 9
U.K. Softcover   ISBN   978 1 4713 3542 6

Printed and bound in Great Britain by TJ International Limited

INTRODUCTION

*If you talk to animals they will talk with you and
you will know each other. If you do not
talk to them you will not know them,
and what you do not know you will fear.
What one fears one destroys.*

Chief Dan George

With the decline of the Pharaohs in Egypt and
the rise and spread of Christianity the sacred
cat became the victim of cruel oppression
rooted in fear

Christianity not only left them out of
the Bible but also allied them with the
devil. Herbalists and Wise Women were
condemned as witches, their cats as familiars.
It was enough for a lonely woman to have a cat
companion and for some trivial occurrence,
such as a neighbour's milk to curdle, for her to
be accused of practising witchcraft and forfeit
her life. Thousands of such women were killed
throughout Europe over a span of several
hundred years, a tragedy not only for them and
their feline friends but for everyone, for with
these women died a vast body of knowledge on
the medicinal use of plants and herbs.

Today Herbalists and Naturopaths are
respected members of society and cats are

much loved in countless households even though they are no longer worshipped as gods—or are they? I, and many others, freely admit that I 'adore' cats. My copy of The Oxford dictionary gives *'worship as divine'* as a meaning for this word.

Cats have a mystic power found in few other creatures; it is this quality that makes some people fear them. They are capable of not just looking at you but through you and deep into your soul.

THE POWER OF THE CAT is not only a tribute to the ones who walked beside me down the years and those who keep me company today but an acknowledgement of the extraordinary charisma and power of all cats everywhere.

1

FIRST LESSONS.

In the beginning God created Man but finding him so feeble, he gave him the cat.

- Warren Eckstein.

I count myself fortunate that when I was born my fairy godmother gave me the gift of an inborn love of cats. A love that was nurtured in my early years by people whose love and understanding of cats almost amounted to worship. They were mostly women, but not, as far as I know, all witches.

Mrs Walters was reputed to be, whether this was true or village gossip I never discovered, I strongly suspect, with the wisdom of hindsight, that she was a witch.

She lived in a little cottage about a quarter of a mile from my home in rural Staffordshire. Set just off the road and reached by a path made dark even in midsummer by overhanging trees and shrubs, the surroundings became even darker when her back door was reached. Yet, astonishingly, she operated a thriving little business from the scullery at the back of her house. Here she sold staples such as biscuits, butter, tea, bread and a surprising range of chocolates and sweets. Everything she sold was good quality. Milk she did not stock, in those days everyone in the village got their milk direct from our dairy or the other farm in the hamlet.

I felt very grown up when my mother deemed me mature enough at four years old to go there by myself and enjoyed the thrill of fear as I ran quickly up the dark path to the even darker backyard. Once at the door all fear left me and I spun out my shopping expedition as long as possible so that I could relish this golden opportunity to meet the cats. All were well fed, and to me they exuded a regal aura. She also had a taciturn little black dog called Carlo. If she had a familiar it was probably Carlo. When he died she buried him under the old Yew tree in the back garden. A stone marked his grave and she told me she had made a shroud for him and put a brand new silver florin inside it with him. I didn't know what a shroud was but I knew that a florin, two shillings, was a great deal of money in the early thirties when I could buy chocolate for as little as a halfpenny. I was too awed to ask the reason for this and it was fifty years later when I was researching old country customs for a book that I discovered that it was the fare for the ferryman to take him across the river Styx to the next world. She did not replace Carlo but one of her cats; a massive long haired black and white called

2

Trix became undisputed leader of her cat family and probably her familiar.

All had simply turned up and stayed. When I asked why they went to her house and not any other, (I would have been ecstatic if they had come to live with us), she simply said. 'They know where to come.'

When I put the same question to my father he explained that when homeless cats need a shelter, temporary or permanent, they looked for the secret sign placed by other cats that told them here was sanctuary.

Mrs Walters was a very old lady, my father had known her when he was a child and said she had been old then. Eighty years or more separated us, but when I admired her cats and she talked about them the age gap dissolved.

Her third husband had died when I was a baby but in her early nineties she married again. Her fourth husband outlived her but although he cared for her cats until they, too, died no new ones joined the group. The secret sign was no longer at her gate.

After her death any wandering cats in the village searching for lodgings turned up at our farmhouse. So at last after a childhood fraught with the deep disappointment, even tragedy, that had accompanied all my attempts to have a close relationship with a cat in the first few years of my life I achieved my dream. My inborn and abiding love for cats had never faltered but had, in fact, been fostered in the unlikely environment of the small boarding school I was sent to a few months before my eighth birthday. Abbotsford School was a genteel private school run by two maiden ladies, Miss Williams and Miss Burton, known of course to their students as Will & Bert. There were only just over a hundred children in the school altogether, of the twenty boarders only nine were there all week. The remainder went home each Friday night and returned on Monday morning. This meant that those of us who were at school at the weekends were more like a large family than a school. Toby and Whiskers added to this family feeling. Toby was Miss William's cat and Miss Burton belonged to Whiskers.

At the weekends all those in residence, had breakfast and mid-day dinner together at a large dining table set in front of the big bay window in the dining room. It was a ritual that never varied.

Plates and the food to be served were placed in front of Miss Williams; on top of the pile of plates were two small bowls, one for each cat. Meanwhile the cats took their places at table along with everyone else. A mat was on the polished floor by Miss William's chair and another at the other end of the table by Miss Burton's chair. Sitting expectantly by each mat was a cat.

They were a handsome pair, both short haired and glossy. Toby's sleek coat was ebony black, Whiskers true silver tabby. At breakfast time porridge or cereal—according to the time of year—was carefully ladled out by Miss Williams into each cat bowl then passed along the table for Miss Burton to add milk. Whisker's bowl was passed down to him and Toby's passed back to Miss Williams.

Once the cats had been fed Miss Williams ladled out breakfast for the teachers, then any senior girls and finally down to myself and the other seven year old. We were the junior members of the weekend family.

This procedure was followed at mid-day dinner, the meat was placed in front of Miss Williams and the vegetables in front of Miss Burton and everybody was served once again in the same order.

The interesting thing about this ritual was that in the five years I was at this school I never heard anyone suggest that anything should be done differently, on the contrary we all, from the teachers down to us very junior children, accepted it as right and proper that the cats should be served first. The cats certainly accepted it as their due, they always behaved perfectly, sitting patiently by their individual mats through grace and the carving of the meat.

We children all loved the cats and I think that it was probably seeing the courtesy with which they were treated that implanted in me a deep respect for all felines and convinced me that though all animals are equal, cats are more equal, to paraphrase George Orwell.

When one of the small family of boarders had a birthday it was the custom for a cake to be sent from home and served at afternoon teatime. The birthday girl, who always returned with a present, carried the first two slices of cake carefully to the large elegant private drawing room where the two ladies and their cats took afternoon tea.

As my birthday was in mid winter I loved to go in there bearing my offering and gaze on what seemed to me a scene of great luxury. Miss Williams and Miss Burton seated either side of a large fire blazing in the marble fireplace, a tea trolley between them, laid with elegant china and a teapot wearing a knitted cosy. Beside each lady sat a cat and in front of each cat was a saucer for his afternoon drink of milk, served just warmed with a dash of tea.

I think the most valuable lesson I learned in my years at this school was the correct way to treat cats. Both had once been unwanted strays and had walked in at different times to adopt the two ladies. Had they seen the secret message, or had these eminently respectable maiden ladies sent out a call on some mystic telegraph?

2

CHOSEN!

*Cats choose you—you have to wait
for them to come to you. -*

Dominic, Cat Man of Key West.

Cats have come into my life in many strange
ways since the summer afternoon when a cat
chose me and altered the course of my life
forever. I didn't realise at the time that the cat
who appeared, apparently from nowhere, and
crossed the grass tennis court straight to me,
shouting a greeting as if we were old buddies
would be one of my greatest teachers. From
her and her successors I learned a great deal
about cats and cat lore, not to mention other
big life lessons. It was my cats who taught
me the nature of true spirituality. It was the
memory of Mrs Muggins that made wonder
seriously about the possibility of reincarnation.

That sultry summer Sunday, relaxing in
a deck chair by the grass court in the large
rambling garden of my childhood home after a
game of tennis my mind was not on anything
deeper than the spasmodic chatter flicking
backwards and forwards between the family.
Every now and then a snore or a sigh from

Becky, our much loved Boxer, punctuated the hum of conversation.

'Wherever has that come from?' My sister's sharp query focused me in the moment.

She was pointing to a black and white cat waddling (she was heavily pregnant) towards us across the grass. She was not coming from the direction of the road and none of us saw her arrive, she was just there, out of the blue. Enquiries in our small community only revealed that no one had ever seen her before. yet she was in good condition and not in the least nervous, even of a large strange dog, now awake and looking at her with as much interest as anyone else in the family.

She gave us all a quick once over, hardly pausing in her advance, then her tail went up in the vertical greeting peculiar to cats, her mouth opened in a pink 'Hello' and speeding up slightly she came straight to me. I bent down and stroked her, she began to purr and rubbed her head against my hand, I picked her up, with difficulty, her body was so round with kitten, and she sat on my lap, her full throttle purring interspersed with happy little cat yelps of sheer happiness.

'You are an ugly old Muggins,' My greeting was rather less than polite 'Where on earth have you come from?' The name stuck, but later I added the courtesy title Mrs

When I thought of myself acquiring a cat of my very own it was invariably a cloyingly sweet chocolate box fluffy kitten. Nothing like the cat who now claimed me as her own.

'You have been chosen—so now you have a cat—or perhaps I should say she has a person.' My father always understood what lay behind the actions of animals. He was silent for a moment before adding; 'I think the secret sign must be at our gate now.'

I nodded, remembering asking why all the stray cats went to Mrs Walters. She had recently died, aged ninety-eight.

The first anything is important—it is the benchmark for everything that follows. The first kiss, the first boy friend—the first cat. The close relationships I have enjoyed down the years with many remarkable cats owe much to Mrs Muggins, who chose me to be her person. She taught me so much about cats in general as well as bigger lessons about love, life and death. Because of her I have always had a very soft spot for black and white cats and cannot imagine how anyone could think them either plain or 'ordinary'. The exception to this I believe were those engaged in the print trade before it was the norm to have colour in the daily papers, they considered black and white cats brought good fortune to a printing enterprise.

Mrs Muggins past remained an enigma. Her unseen, unheralded arrival together with her excellent physical condition and the calm demeanour, she displayed showing no concern whatever about either strange humans or dogs, only added to the mystery. We suspected that her pregnancy led to owners she trusted taking her for a car trip and dumping her. I wonder if they ever gave a thought to the outcome of such a callous act.

Ten days later she had her kittens, conveniently in the loft above my pony's stable so that I discovered them almost immediately. In those days before it became the accepted thing to de-sex cats the recognised method of stopping them breeding to plague proportions was to destroy female kittens at birth. Muggins was left with two male kittens. A black and white whose back was marked exactly like the six side of a dice; six large black spots marched in two by two formation down his white back. He grew up into a very handsome cat, also an exceedingly lazy one. I called him Spot and his litter brother, a short haired tabby with white bib and paws, Tiggy.

The naming of cats wrote T.S. Elliot *is a difficult matter,*

It isn't just one of your holiday games;

It was obviously, judging by the banality of the names I chose, too difficult for me.

I spent as long in the hayloft crooning over them as Muggins did herself and could only stare, in icy horror when I found the box empty. At three weeks old they were incapable of fending for themselves. Could they have clambered out of the box? I searched every inch of the hayloft. There was no sign or sound of them. Back down the ladder I searched the stables expecting, and dreading, the discovery of two tiny mutilated bodies, killed when they fell on the cobbled floor. Or worse were trampled by the iron shod hooves of my pony. Not a whisker to be seen. Nor could I hear the faintest squeak of hungry kittens. Only the contented munching as my pony pulled at her hay.

My sympathy for the bereaved mother waned when, apparently not in the least concerned, she merely blinked at me and purred when I demanded an explanation. When I had her under surveillance she was about the place as much as normal, apparently unconcerned about her babies; but I could not watch her twenty-four hours a day.

I labelled her a cruel heartless mother who did not care one whit about the fate of her offspring. Those who said cats were cold, calculating and totally selfish were right after all. I am ashamed to say that I was the one who became distant and cool to the point of icy, barely able to respond with civility to her overtures. Muggins, for her part behaved as she had ever since she walked into my life, with courtesy and affection.

Three weeks after their disappearance my father was on one of his customary walks round the farm and was a mile or more from the house, about as far as possible yet still within our boundary. To his astonishment he saw Mrs Muggins sitting in a hedgerow watching her kittens, now considerably grown, playing in the sun. He picked them up and put one in each side pocket of his old tweed jacket, had a little talk with Muggins, so he told me, and with her babies safely in his pockets Muggins trotted along with him beside the dogs, back home.

'I just told her there was no need to worry, I had no intention of hurting them and they really would be better at the house.' My father explained after he had told us where he found them. We settled the little family in a comfortable bed in the house. We had got the message; in future her kittens were born indoors and she never felt it necessary to remove any again.

Mrs Muggins was the embodiment of the two aspects of the great cat goddess of Ancient Egypt. The friendly diminutive, Puss is probably a corruption of the name Pasht the warm household goddess often shown with kittens. In her fiercer side, the hunter, the 'tearer and renderer' known as Sekhmet, she is usually depicted as lion-headed to emphasise her power. It was this aspect of the cat that I learned so much about from Muggins.

She was a skilful hunter; it had obviously been quite easy for her to keep Tiggy and Spot well fed in the weeks she kept them away from us. If she hoped to instil in them the same ability she failed. Both turned out useless in this respect. As did all her kittens except her last two; maybe because by this time her own powers were waning. She was such a good provider for her earlier kittens they saw no need to do anything for themselves.

She brought a constant supply of half-grown rabbits, which she skinned neatly. She also caught sparrows and as the kittens developed, mice for them and rats for us. She neither ate the latter nor offered them to her kittens. These offerings, always placed on the doormat first thing in the morning, were exclusively for us. One morning I opened the back door to see no less than five rats laid out neatly, all their heads in the same direction. One, which I took to be the mother, was almost double the size of the other four. Obviously they were a complete family. My father, who had a high regard for the inner feelings of animals, insisted that whoever was the finder of these early morning gifts should courteously thank her before removing them. He was correct; it is considered social etiquette in the cat world to show appreciation for food and to contribute to the family larder.

Because he liked to boast of her prowess in the pub and point out to his farming friends how much more efficient she was than any other form of rat control, her reputation grew and her kittens were in demand. It was wonderful to have homes for kittens in a world full of surplus cats so we never admitted that Tiggy and Spot had grown up the laziest pair of couch potatoes in all catdom. One of her sons went to the local grocer ostensibly to deal with the mice in his storeroom. A handsome long haired cat he led a very pleasant life sitting on a chair in the grocer's shop basking in the admiration of customers, far too grand to deal with the mice in the storeroom.

My father kept a tally of Muggins' rat kills; there was never a month in which her total dropped below twenty. In fact her average was often one a day. It was probably because she was such a good provider for her offspring that they saw no need to do anything themselves.

Tiggy was so averse to hunting that when the threshing machine turned up and all the cats made for the haystacks he fled for the house and the comfort of the kitchen rocking chair. Tiggy had very odd taste buds for a cat, he loved tomatoes and if a salad was left on the table and no one noticed him snoozing in the rocking chair he would steal the tomatoes and slices of hard-boiled egg from it. He once climbed to the very topmost shelf of the pantry, so high one needed a stepladder to reach things stored there, and ate steadily through half a bag of dried fruit my mother was hoarding for her Christmas cake and pudding. This was in the post war days when such luxuries as dried fruit were still in short supply.

14

Muggins' generous offer of a large freshly killed rat was not appreciated by my mother. One summer morning, she was in what we called the second pantry skimming the cream off a bowl of milk, and as it was mid summer the outside door was open. I heard 'Hello, Mug,' in a pleasant conversational voice followed by a piercing scream. Muggins had laid her gift carefully across my mother's bare foot in open sandals.

When she was a very old cat with few teeth my father at the window saw her emerge from the stable with a full-grown rat in her mouth. He grabbed the poker on his way out intending to kill it before she was injured. She placed the body on the ground in front of him, surprised and pleased at such enthusiasm, He bent down and picked it up cautiously by the tail. It was quite dead, her one remaining sharp incisor had pierced its throat in exactly the crucial spot.

I was impressed by the old cat's self control when I came across her in the backyard, pausing now and then in what seemed a rather casual toilet, to glance at a very young chicken. It had somehow escaped from the metal brooder heated by a paraffin lamp in the nearby shed where I was rearing a hundred pullets, one day old when they arrived a week before. She miaowed at me in some concern, obviously telling me that I really should take better care of them, and watched me catch it and return it to its tin mother. I was amazed for she had kittens at the time and could well have been excused if she saw this as a tasty snack for them and far easier to catch than a sparrow.

I grew to love Muggins dearly for herself but it was her ability as a hunter that first commanded our respect. Several thousand years ago it was this aspect of the cat that first led to her becoming one of the greatest deities in Ancient Egypt. For all their religion and mysticism the Egyptians were also very practical people; they recognised the value of the cat in protecting their precious grain stores.

Today this part of cat nature is reviled rather than respected but when I was a child on an English farm it was the most important. It is interesting to note that whenever this hunting skill of cats has been ignored it has been disastrous for humans.

When the Black Death reached Europe the Pope, Clement VI actually promoted the ritual killing of cats. This decimation of the feline population resulted in huge increase in rat numbers who were carriers of the disease and so caused the spread of the plague to be even more virulent.

A similar thing happened in Japan in the Middle Ages when a cat-loving emperor issued a decree that cats should no longer be expected to work. An infestation of mice in the silk industry caused this to be repealed.

Undoubtedly the recognition of the cat's remarkable achievements in keeping down the rodent population in grain stores was a leading factor in the spread of the Roman Empire for they carried cats on their ships and in doing so introduced domestic cats to the lands they settled in, including Britain.

Howel the Good, a prince in central Wales in the 11th.Century made laws known as the Gwentian Code. This gave cats protection and legal status and also made their owners responsible for their behaviour. He put a monetary value on cats. One penny for a newborn kitten, two pennies when it had killed its first mouse and four pence for a mature cat with all its claws, teeth, sight and hearing, and if a female, a careful nurse. The penalty for stealing or killing a cat was commensurate with its value. The owner must be compensated with either a ewe and her lamb or enough grain to completely cover the body of the cat when it was held by the tip of its tail with its nose just touching the ground.

Muggins would have been a valuable asset to any farmer in those days, as indeed she was to us. Many cats are efficient mousers but one prepared to tackle and kill a full-grown rat is much more rare.

Her influence on us as a family was profound. She turned my dog-loving parents into cat lovers and she confirmed my inborn

17

liking into an abiding love and a deep respect, I wanted to know more cats personally and to find out a lot more about them as a species.

I have noticed in life how often the most unexpected things, people, events can have a profound effect on the course of one's life. If anyone had told me that summer afternoon when a stray black and white cat, with no claim to either beauty or breeding, appeared out of nowhere to claim me as a friend, that she would, through her daughter, Gussie, launch me into the absorbing world of Cat Shows and pedigree cats, I would have laughed at the idea. Yet looking back down the long vista of the years I can see my meeting with this eminently lovable cat as crucial to the course my life would take. It was, though I did not realise it at the time, the power of the cat in action.

Not only did I get to know a great many cats and their people personally, but delving into the intriguing history of this amazing species as well as learning something of their status in the modern world led to the publication of my first full length book and my first radio broadcast, both about cats.

3

WHITE CATS ARE MORE EQUAL

An idea of aristocracy was suggested by her elegance and distinction.

Théophile Gautier—about his white cat, Seraphita.

We all have 'Ah-Ha' moments in life, peak experience when we 'see' something clearly. My first sight of Gussie was one of these.

I held the tiny white kitten in my hand. As I stared at the pink lips, bright pink nose, pink ears and, most amazing of all the pink paws which looked incredibly like tiny human hands time stopped for a heartbeat and I knew that the God I had believed in since childhood, the bearded old man in the sky, did not exist. What did was something far more awesome, a Great Spirit, an all embracing life force, who had not just created the kitten but was part of it. We were both, the kitten and I, part of the same great whole, neither necessarily more valuable than the other. This brief moment changed my thinking forever. God was never again for me someone 'out there', but the life force in every living thing, making us all fragments of the divine.

From the moment I first held the tiny white kitten in my hand I adored white cats; I yearned for more of them, and I wanted to learn about them. Muggins was a very old cat when she had these last kittens, not a litter but a 'pigeon pair'. A male, just like her and a white female, not, I thought at the time, pure white for she had two black smudges on top of her head. Two months before her birth a magnificent large white tom cat with blazing amber eyes had appeared briefly in the village. His legacy was three white kittens, two males born to a cat belonging to a neighbour and the tiny female in my hand.

I do not believe either chance or coincidence order our lives but we are led, not driven, by unseen guides. We are given choices; what we choose is up to us. This was the only daughter from Muggins to survive our policy of only rearing male kittens; I could have chosen to ignore the flash of enlightenment when I first held her in my hand; instead I chose to keep her and changed the course of my life. Angels don't always have wings.   I called her Gussie, after Gorgeous Gussie Moran, the glamorous star of Wimbledon that year. Through her I discovered the world of pedigree cats, made many new friends, had my first book published, did my first radio broadcast and gave my first public talk, I hesitate to use the word 'lecture', to Oxford Cat Club appropriately on the subject of white cats.

Cats of every shade and shape have enriched my life, not only my own but those of other people. White cats have played a significant part, often influencing crucial decisions that changed the direction my life would take.

Writing is a notoriously dicey profession: for every one who makes a fortune more barely exist.. Many, like me, choose to learn in the university of life. It was at this time when I was trying to establish myself as a freelance journalist that I took a live-in position as a Nanny. My charges were eighteen month old twins and my employer, the commanding officer at a large R.A.F. base. With Gussie in the care of my parents, who both adored her, I embarked on one of the bleakest and loneliest spells of my life and met another remarkable white cat. Through him my life once again changed direction.

I was supposed to live *en famille* but my employers seldom addressed more than a *pass the mustard* type of sentence to me; the children did not eat with their parents and at eighteen months old were not brilliant conversationalists. The two R.A.F. personnel employed as batmen to run the household were friendly enough but I was told that I was not to fraternise with them. There were other nannies employed by the officers and they got together and took their charges out in their prams each afternoon. I was told I could not join them, they probably thought I might gossip about what went on in the C.O's household. All this added up to acute loneliness from which I was saved by a white cat whose name I never learned, he was just 'the cat', as I was just 'the Nanny'.

He was a beautiful cat, a large and handsome white neutered male. He obviously knew the layout of the house and I had barely settled into my room upstairs at the back, where the roofs sloped down over the kitchen area, when he appeared outside my bedroom window. He peered in and politely asked me to open it. This I did and we immediately formed a friendship based on fellow feeling. He never asked me to open the door so that he could enter the rest of the house but left me late at night, sometimes in the early hours, the same way he had come in.

He was unfailingly polite and friendly but although I talked to him a great deal about my gripes with my situation he did not tell me anything about himself. I learned his story on one of the rare occasions I had an opportunity for a brief conversation with one of the batmen.

He had, as I suspected, lived in this house as the much-loved pet of the previous C.O. and his wife. When they received an overseas posting they asked my employers if they would keep the cat. This they agreed to do.

'If they had known that he would not be allowed in the house I think they would have tried to find another home for him,' the batmen said, 'The only thing they do for him is tell me to feed him once a day. So I do—the best of their meat and stuff—I feel sorry for him; after all this was his home for three years, and they agreed to let him stay.' He obviously thought the cat had been shabbily treated, I agreed.

I had been there barely six weeks, long enough to form a close friendship with my nightly visitor when the Group Captain said to his wife across the lunch table;

'You'll be pleased to know I've found someone to take on that cat, they are collecting him this afternoon.'

His wife, who was fanatical about keeping germs and babies separate, may have been pleased but I was not. I handed in my notice the following day. I cannot remember what reason I gave, not the truth, that the place was unbearable without my feline friend.

If I hadn't left this job I probably would not have ended up working in London where I met the man I would marry, with the approval of yet another white cat. It seemed that every time I came to a crossroad in my life a white cat was there to help me make the right decision.

I don't count sheep at night—I review past events and scan in my mind the fascinating way one leads to another, rather like the clues in a treasure hunt.

When I returned home, feeling a bit like the flotsam and jetsam washed up on a friendly beach I was grateful for my father's offer to employ me himself. He offered me the job of rearing calves and looking after poultry, both of which I enjoyed. It was in this period in my life that I discovered the fascinating world of pedigree cats, and it was Gussie who led me there.

She was now a mature cat having kittens of her own, fifty percent of every litter were white. To my surprise these were in demand, so much so that people wanted to pay for them. Obviously more people thought white cats beautiful than were concerned about them being unlucky. When I discovered two small independent magazines devoted entirely to cats I also learned that they did indeed have a commercial value.

What is more short haired white cats, like Gussie were a recognised breed and cats who came up to the standard as laid down by the Governing Council of the Cat Fancy could be registered in the supplementary register and three generations later become pedigree cats.

I was not the only one who felt there was something inherently superior about Gussie, apart from herself, she was the first cat allowed full house cat status by my mother. She was not confined to the kitchen area or even downstairs but had the run of the entire house. My father admired her intellect and suspected that she either understood English or had psychic powers when she was discovered stripping the wallpaper off the spare bedroom wall immediately after someone on television had described his cat doing that very thing.

I began to wonder about her antecedents, not just the splendid white male whose brief appearance in the village had left such a legacy but about white cats in general.

The first white cats known in Europe were long haired, they were introduced to Italy in the sixteenth century and from there to France. They were known as Angoras as they came originally from Ankara in Turkey. They were fine boned, almost invariably white and had pointed faces and largish ears. Their coat was silky rather than woolly.

Fittingly as the Church leaders had caused cats so much suffering by linking them to witchcraft and the devil, it was eminent churchmen and men of letters who did much to raise the status of cats. Cardinal Richelieu was a passionate cat lover and at his death left pensions for those he had. In a real turn around for the cat there were even popes who made no secret of their love for cats.

Chateaubriand not only loved cats but wrote charmingly about what he called his White dynasty. Nowadays Angoras as a breed have vanished. When cat shows and breeding became popular in England they were indiscriminately crossed with the long haired cats imported from what was then known as Persia. These cats had heavier bone, denser more woolly coats, broader skulls, shorter noses and smaller ears. Blue and black were the predominant colours although they could be any of the many different cat colours. In this cross breeding the Angora characteristics were lost in Show cats with the exception of the white coat colour, and the name was dropped; all long haired cats became known as Persians.

Every white cat must have at least one white parent so if I could have gone back far enough through the generations behind Gussie I would have eventually come to these imported aristocrats and the reason for her undoubted specialness. But can anything be totally lost? When I look through old photos and see pictures of Sheba, the white cat who lived with me here in Australia, or look at Lily who shares my home today, they could be any of the nineteenth century Angoras in my old cat books.

Tiny, the white cat I bought from a Scottish breeder, always had a slightly too long coat even though she was third generation short hair breeding. This powerful cat, in terms of personality, (physically she was small and frail), was one of my greatest teachers responsible for the opening of my mind and heart. I had loved other cats but my feeling for them had been more as a mother for her child rather than as an equal. I had loved them as, I thought, one should love pets. A word I feel is demeaning to them now. I loved Tiny as my friend and my equal. In my youthful arrogance I can remember wondering if my relationship with Tiny was unique, and thinking it was, that other people did not have such a close bond with their animals. Now I know that many people feel this and that I was not alone in recognising the spirituality of other, non-human beings.

When Tiny left me to cross the rainbow bridge she taught me that death is just that, a moving from one plane to another, a temporary parting.

Many years later in Australia I met Sheba, another remarkable white cat in my life, destined to teach me more about death and dying and life beyond death. Almost as if she had come to continue where Tiny left off.

I was surprised to find that many people considered white cats unlucky. I lost count of the number of times the old proverb *'Kiss the black cat and grow fat; kiss the white cat and grow lean'* was quoted at me.

The second thing I learned about white cats was about the black smudges I had considered blemishes on Gussie's head when she was born. By weaning age these were fading and long before she reached maturity they had vanished completely.

I knew that the deafness that occurs in many white cats was not a myth or a superstition but a hereditary defect tied to the gene for white coat colour. It does not, however as some people believe, occur in all white cats.

White cats can have yellow, orange, or blue eyes, or odd eyes, one yellow. one blue. The deafness more often manifests in blue-eyed cats but not always; where it does occur is in those cats born without the black smudges. I call these marks smudges because that is what they appear to be. Exactly as if one, two or even three fingers have been dipped in soot and then placed on the kitten's head. Breeders of white cats eagerly look for these celestial guarantees of perfect hearing. I never had a kitten born without them, nor did I have one who retained them beyond kittenhood, or one who was deaf, whatever the colour of their eyes.

I have often wondered at the superstition prevalent in England that white cats are unlucky. For me they always seemed special and I was not surprised to discover when researching the role of cats in other cultures that far from being thought of as unlucky they are held in the highest esteem.

Whether I was performing a service for cats in general when I transformed my moggies into aristo-cats is debatable, but for me these years were a steep learning curve in cat lore.

I read avidly, everything I could lay my hands on about cats, and met many wonderful human friends who generously shared their knowledge with me and even more remarkable cats who became part of my life.

4

CATS ON VIEW

'Even the smallest feline is a work of art.'

Leonardo da Vinci

I had discovered a newsprint weekly called FUR & FEATHER. In addition to news about rabbits and birds it had a large cat section with reports on cat shows, including the judge's comments on each cat. I was amazed to discover that 'ordinary' tabbies were not ordinary at all if they had no white markings and had the correct stripes, blodges and swirls superimposed on a ground colour of silver, red, or sable. One of our current family of cats was a handsome tabby with all the required markings on his rich brown coat unspoilt by any odd patches of white. He had a wonderful temperament and had not been de-sexed .

It was a simple matter to launch into cat breeding, All I had to do was register Tim and

Gussie with the Governing Council of The Cat Fancy and let them do the rest.

I awaited the arrival of my first almost pedigree kittens eagerly; only two more generations and they would be out of the Supplementary Register and in 'The Book'. I spent these waiting weeks studying every word I could find on the physical attributes of a good show cat. I learned that good Brown Tabbies were actually quite hard to find. It was not just the markings that were so important, a distinct M on the head, swirls across the cheeks from the corners of the eyes, unbroken necklaces and bracelets round the legs. They must have a head 'round as an apple', large luminous eyes, and medium sized ears. The colour and quality of the coat was of prime importance. A plush texture was desirable in a deep sable brown with no hint of grey. Physically the cat should be cobby rather than svelte.

When Gussie had her kittens, two brown tabbies and two whites, I was over the moon and studied them critically with the eyes of an expert, rather newly to be sure, but an expert for all that. I planned to make my début in the show world at the big kitten show held in London each summer as a breeder of white cats but my newly acquired knowledge and critical eye told me that the brace of white kittens I inended to enter were really quite ordinary; the tabbies on the other hand, especially the female, were almost perfect examples of their breed. I sold the two whites and entered the tabbies in the Show. There would be more kittens from Tim and Gussie and next time it might be the whites who were show cats.

So much for plans. There were no more kittens; Gussie developed ovarian cysts and had to be spayed and Tim was caught in a rabbit snare and developed septicaemia which failed to respond to any of the drugs available at the time and died. Here Fate stepped in again,

By a stroke of good fortune the printers left the words FOR SALE out of the catalogue. The male was sold before the show, for an amazing five guineas, the two whites I had sold for two guineas each; the buyer had obtained his details from the Cat Fancy and bought him sight unseen. She agreed to let him remain with me until after the Show. To my delight I discovered their pen covered with award cards when I returned to the hall after the judging. This was the entrée to a distinguished show career for Tabitha Twitchet, the female. She became a full Champion while still a very young adult. She and I were both hooked; I never had another cat that loved shows so much. She was a natural extrovert and wallowed in the attention. One judge wrote in her report *'This cat was a joy to handle—she never stopped purring.'*

The photographer, who had been sent by the editor of the local paper, for whom apparently, cat shows were as much a novelty as they were to me, placed her on the table with her prize cards around her; 'Can't you stop her posing?' he complained 'She doesn't look natural.' I couldn't, and she appeared in the paper smiling smugly at the camera.

She loved nothing better than an audience. Perhaps she had been an actress in a previous incarnation, in this life the show hall was her theatre. Like any good performer she could hold her audience in thrall as I discovered at the National Show, the feline equivalent of Crufts, in the huge Olympia Hall in London.

I had given her a bowl of minced beef and taken a stroll round to look at the other exhibits; on my return the crowd was so dense round her pen that I couldn't get near her. Every now and then a chuckle of delight erupted from this audience. What on earth was Tabitha up to?

When I finally fought my way to the front of the crowd I saw an intriguing performance. Tabitha was sitting, not standing, in front of her dish, very elegantly she put her paw in the minced meat and transferred a piece to her mouth, then looked expectantly at the crowd, this was when they 'Oohed' and 'Aahed' and chuckled with pleasure, some even clapped.

I was stunned, I had never seen her do this before. Loving her food she was always in a hurry to eat her meals. This was obviously a party trick specially designed to amuse her fans at a Show. She turned round and saw me, and looked anything but pleased. The impromptu performance ceased and her glare told me very clearly that I was not wanted at that moment. 'Go away—push off,' she said quite rudely, 'you are spoiling my act.'

Her audience turned as one in my direction and someone asked if I owned her. I saw Tabitha's eyes glint at that, anyone knew who did the owning. I left her to her audience.

I would look at her sometimes and wonder how I had ever considered tabbies ordinary. Those dramatic black swirls across her cheeks and the clear M on her head that legend said proclaimed the cat's connection with Mohamed. He had loved and admired them proclaiming them clean animals and as such fit to enter the mosque. There are many legends and stories connecting the prophet with cats, once, it is said he cut off the sleeve of his robe rather than disturb his cat who was asleep on it when it was time for him to go to prayer. He is also credited with bestowing on the cat the ability to land on her feet when falling from a height.

The chain of events that began when a funny lovable old cat waddled across a summer lawn and chose me, now led me into a new world, with new friends and a fascinating hobby. It also launched me as an author. I had always loved writing and had some small successes with articles and even the occasional short story, but when I began writing about cats fresh doors opened. I saw all this as fortunate happenstance at the time not as the mystical power of the cat weaving its potent magic in the fabric of my life.

5

ARISTO-CATS ALL

With tail erect and pompous march, the proudest puss that ever trod.—

Lytton Strachey

I like to think that with the advancing years my wisdom quotient, if not my I.Q., has increased, or at least evolved. Today I question the ethics of breeding cats with snobbish bloodlines when shelters everywhere are full of beautiful cats and kittens needing homes. Many of these will be killed. Not—as people like to say 'put to sleep'. There is no waking in this dimension for them.

The cat's curse is her fecundity; if cats gave birth to one kitten every two years instead of two litters a year of five or six kittens each, their place in the world would be assured.

The advance in veterinary surgery has made it possible to control the cat population by de-sexing; The Ancient Egyptians, who revered the cat, had a unique way of solving this over population problem.

When thousands of mummified cats were discovered in Egypt there were newborn kittens among them posing the question, why were there were so many kittens? A large proportion appear to have died with broken necks, in a community that revered cats to such an extent that they had elevated them to deity status this seemed an anomaly.

Pious worshippers of the cat goddess believed they could gain special help from her by purchasing a sacrificial offering in the form of a kitten, possibly born within the temple precincts. Such a practice would have a threefold benefit. First, and most obviously, it would help the temple coffers, secondly it would boost faith in, and veneration for, the great cat deity and finally it would prevent a population explosion amongst the cats themselves.

When I pulled my own cats up the feline social scale, I gave them a place and a value in the world. Now they were aristocats, not alley cats, I never had the slightest problem selling kittens for fair prices to good homes. More people than I had imagined loved and appreciated tabby cats. Far from questioning the ethics of what I was doing I saw myself as occupying the moral high ground

In what, at the time, seemed a series of frustrations bordering on the disastrous, my attempts to breed white cats were baulked at every turn while my tough little Brownies were smiled on by the gods. Gussie never had another litter, when she failed to conceive and lost weight dramatically the vet diagnosed ovarian cysts and told me that if I wanted to save her life she would have to be spayed. She was seven years old at the time. The operation was a great success, she lived a happy healthy life for another ten years, but of course no more kittens. The little white cat I had bought from a Scottish breeder had her first litter by Tim, two very mediocre whites and a truly beautiful brown tabby, Tiberius. He grew up to have the most amazing eyes, huge and round and a wonderful aquamarine in colour. It was as if the blue eyes on his mother's side and the yellow of his father had been blended like paint to produce this fantastic colour. I thought him far too good to sell as a neutered pet and kept him to breed from. He like Tabitha earned the right at a very early age to put Ch. in front of his name.

Tabitha's eldest daughter, Peggy Sue, a very well marked Tortoiseshell, sired by a well-known Champion Red Tabby, followed in her mother's paw prints and quickly became a champion for her new owner. The reflected glory I wallowed in with three Champions carrying my prefix was some compensation for the fact that they were not white.

True tortoiseshell cats are interesting; their coats are a blend of black, red and cream, which is the dilute form of red. One might expect it to be genetically unlikely if not impossible for normal and dilute coat colour to appear in the same animal. A good Tortoiseshell is born almost black and the red and cream comes through slowly. There were two torties in Tabitha's first litter, fortunately I knew this about the colouring, the one that looked near perfect at birth ended up far too light while the one that was almost black was a perfect colour at maturity; I was pleased when she was bought by a breeder. Tortie and white cats are a mixture of black and orange with white markings. Like tortoiseshells they are always female, they, however are born with their adult coat colour and pattern. Country people in Northern England value these cats believing they are powerful talismans to keep the homestead safe from the ravages of fire.

Tabitha was my entrée to the world of pedigree cats and cat shows; together we travelled to shows all over England. She stayed with me in the homes of friends and relations and in the best Hotels; always the best for they did not query the travelling case that sometimes miaowed when taken to my room. For the same reason I travelled first class on the train. Her tremendous enjoyment of these trips and all about them showed me a facet of cat character I had not thought existed and helped to make them immensely enjoyable.

She was a very pretty cat and had a charm and charisma that owed as much to her character as her conformation. The word ordinary never crossed my mind now when I looked at her rich sable coat with its intricate pattern of ebony stripes and splodges. Her brick red nose was cute in the middle of her head, round as an apple as the show standard required, but best of all were her huge round eyes, light gold and bright like peridot and always so full of expression; I wondered where the word tabby originated and discovered that at one time fashionable ladies were often described as 'wearing a gown of tabby silk', a form of watered silk, posing a classical *which came first question;* Was the silk named after the cat or visa versa?

I would look at Tabitha sometimes and wonder if Mohammed's cat had been a tabby like her, the one for whom he was reputed to have cut off the sleeve of his robe rather than disturb her slumbers. The dark mark over a tabby's shoulders is believed to be the imprint of the prophet's hand.

Tabitha's great charm lay largely in her uninhibited enjoyment of life. She was both lovable and loving. A joy to look at and enormous fun to have around. Quite by accident, I discovered that she enjoyed being vacuumed. She was getting in my way when I was cleaning the lounge suite with the attachment for that purpose, so I put the nozzle on her back and ran it down her spine, intending to deter her. Instead she arched towards it in ecstasy and when I flicked the off switch the noise of the vacuum was replaced by her loud purring. After that I vacuumed her regularly.

Bathing cats was something I never envisioned doing until the day before we left home for Tabitha's second show; leaning over the edge to steal a drink she fell head first into a bucket half full of milk. Shampooing was the easiest way to get her clean. She appeared to enjoy this as much as being vacuumed; her black and sable coat came up as if polished, the black markings appearing superimposed, so after that a bath before a show became the norm.

If I left her outside the bathroom when I was in the tub she yelled and scrabbled at the door making relaxation as I soaked difficult so I usually let her in with me. She actually fell in with me more than once. In view of her own enjoyment of a bath I suspected it might not have been entirely accidental. It always happened in the same way, picking her way round the rim of the bath she leaned too close to me to tell me what fun this was and splash, she was in with me! Curiously enough the only other cat to fall in the bath with me was another Tabitha, many years and a world away in the future.

She had an insatiable curiosity and gave a whole new dimension to the saying 'Curiosity killed the cat.' Because she took good care of the inner cat and was never late for meals, when she was late for her dinner I was sure something was wrong. I called her inside the house and outside. I searched every possible place then I remembered I had been up to the attic on the third floor searching for something in the stored jumble. It was cut off from the rest of the house by a door. I reclimbed the tortuous stairs and peered round,

'Tabitha?' I heard, or imagined I heard, a faint muffled answer. 'Tabitha are you there?" I stood still and listened; I could hear something but it wasn't Tabitha's clear voice. I finally tracked the sound to a pile of cardboard boxes saved for some unexpected eventuality in the future. By leaning towards it and listening carefully I traced the faint voice to a long cardboard tube. Reaching as far as my arm would go I was just able to grab the end of what I guessed, and fervently hoped, was Tabitha's tail. I pulled—hard; the body attached to the tail was firmly wedged. I pulled harder and out she came, rear end first, mouth open, gasping for breath.

I don't know how much longer she would have survived; there was no way she could possibly have extricated herself. She wasn't as grateful as I felt she should be, no doubt afraid of losing face, and explained virtuously that she was looking for mice.

Until I had Tabitha I had no idea that cats, as well as kittens, could be so much fun and such enchanting companions. If nothing else she taught me the important lesson that cats, no less than people, come with all sorts of personalities, their greatest quality being their individualism.

Her kittens were beautiful and always in demand both by breeders and those who just wanted a pet. She was a good but not over zealous or devoted mother, when she had kittens within a few days of Tiny, the little white cat from Scotland, who became her best friend, she took full advantage of the situation. Each afternoon about two pm. Tabitha picked up her four kittens one at a time and transferred them to Tiny's basket, placing them carefully with the three already there. Then off she went to spend the afternoon enjoying herself in her usual frivolous manner. Dutifully Tiny curled round all seven kittens and mothered them till Tabitha returned, collected her babies and took them back to her own bed.

The success of my Brownies had not lessened my desire to breed beautiful white cats, preferably with blue eyes. Following this dream I had bought Tiny from a Scottish breeder. Both parents and all four

41

grandparents were blue-eyed, I had seen one of her grandfathers at a London Show; he was a well-known and well-deserved champion with brilliant sky blue eyes, a sparkling plush white coat and perfect hearing. Tiny alas was odd eyed, one brilliant blue eye and one yellow but I felt that with such antecedents she must produce blue eyed kittens. She never did but became the mother of a very special Brown Tabby Champion.

This diminutive feline had more guts and character packed inside her small body than I could ever have imagined when I unpacked the cardboard box in which she had travelled all the way from Aberdeen on the overnight express train.

When the student is ready—the teacher arrives. My teacher had come; to teach me among other lessons about Life, Love and Death that the true value of cats has nothing to do with their success in the Show Hall, nor even in the grace and beauty of their physical appearance. The power of the cat lies in its spirit; its ability to live in two dimensions, its capacity to love and a certain inner wisdom available on tap for those who have open minds and hearts.

6

ONE BLUE EYE

His eyes look as if he's pawned his real ones...

Russell Hoban

'My God—she's tiny!' My mother was the first to break the silence as I opened the cardboard box on the kitchen table and drew out the little scrap of fur who far from cowering in the bottom of the box was staring at us with startling odd eyes, one golden yellow the other a brilliant sapphire blue.

I put my hand in the box and felt bones through a harsh coat, not the soft silky one of a healthy kitten. Her pot belly betrayed the presence of internal parasites and the black specks of flea excreta on her coat external ones.

With that first shocked exclamation my mother gave her the name she would be known by for her entire life, Tiny. It certainly suited her far better than her registered pedigree name, *Whitehaugh Cream Cracker*. She stared calmly into my face with those extraordinary eyes; I stared back, noticing the leonine chin and the small hooked nose suggesting an unusually strong character. I had collected

43

her from her caretakers at a London Show re-packed for another train journey to the English Midlands so this was my first face-to-face meeting with the incredible character who was to become my deeply loved friend and companion, my courageous and wise teacher for the next ten years. As a very small tribute to her I dedicated my book, *Cats' Company'* *'To the memory of Tiny, best beloved of all my company of cats.'*

My practical mother swung immediately into action, she spread newspaper over the table and got the flea comb, within minutes she had removed nineteen fleas from the pathetically small body, keeping count in between her dark mutterings about just what she would like to do to the person who could let a kitten get in this state, then have the nerve to charge for her. And compound the felony by sending her off on the overnight express from Scotland to London in a tatty old cardboard box. A totally inadequate container that any normal fit kitten would have escaped from long before the train crossed the border into England.

'What did the person who met her off the train in London have to say about her?' she demanded at the conclusion of her monosyllabic muttering.

'I hope you can rear her.' I replied truthfully.

'We are damn well going to!' My mother

assured me as she screwed up the paper with its nineteen dead fleas and threw it in the fire. 'Now we had better give her some nourishment.'

Even after the fleas and then the worms were dealt with it took three months of intensive care and the help of a very good veterinarian before she was out of the woods. First she went down with enteritis and lost even more weight, then the hair on her body all fell out. This was mid-winter in England but fortunately we had a solid fuel stove that was kept alight twenty four hours a day throughout the winter. She had a cosy bed close to it and never left the room until she had a full coat again.

I was awed by her determination to live and humbled by her confidence. Her experience in her three months of living cannot have given her cause for such optimism. Many times I crept down in the middle of the night to make sure she was warm and still alive. So many times we were convinced that not even her indomitable spirit could keep her alive.

But my mother also had immense determination One afternoon she took off in the car without a word and came back with a jar of Brand's chicken essence and two jars of chicken baby food. The essence encouraged her failing appetite and the baby food kept her going till she was strong enough to eat bits of chicken, steak and sardines.

For three months she was the focal point of the household, even our kind Boxer bitch contributed to her care. Becky liked to lie stretched out on her side with her belly facing the stove. She allowed Tiny to climb over her body and settle herself between her legs, her back against the comforting belly of the big dog and the warmth of the stove radiating onto her own small frame. I think as well as warmth she received healing strength and comfort from the dog.

She was destined to be my friend and companion, my inspiration and my guru for ten eventful years in my life. Always frail in body she radiated the power of the cat as an inner, spiritual quality.

Still obsessed by my ambition to breed perfect blue-eyed whites I felt at eighteen months old Tiny was mature and fit enough to breed, even though she was now precious for herself, not her potential to produce champions. The only short haired white cat at stud was her grandfather up in Scotland so I decided to send her to a good British Blue Shorthair. She was returned to me un-mated. The stud owner explained apologetically that she had been so traumatised by the journey and was so small and frail she was afraid to put her in with him. So, like Gussie before her I let her stay home and have a litter by Tim, Tabitha's father. These were his last kittens before his untimely death. Once more I had two very ordinary white kittens and one of the loveliest tabby males I had ever seen. What made him so striking was his remarkable eyes, they were large and expressive in a perfectly marked round face and were an extraordinary aquamarine colour. Once more the white kittens went off into the world as pets and I chose to keep Tiberius. He had an exceptional temperament and a distinguished show career rapidly gaining the awards that made him a full champion.

The following year Tiny returned to the handsome Blue cat whose owner had been so understanding and came back in kitten. She had three kittens, two white males and a pure black female. All were sold as pets. Her next litter by the same cat reversed this, two white females and a black male. One of the females was top quality and went to a breeder, the other two kittens went as pets. Not one of her white kittens could rustle up even one blue eye between them. Candy, who went down to Devon for breeding, had the lovely copper eyes of her father. Had I looked in my crystal ball and seen that Tiny would never have any more kittens I would have kept Candy. However destiny would bring us together again. But that was a long way in the future.

I was walking along the garden path on my way to the peas, when one of the cats following me pounced on Tiny and she hit the side of her head against the pointed corner of one of the bricks set at an angle to make an edging for a garden bed.

She righted herself but appeared to have lost her sense of balance. By evening she was worse, not better, she fell off her chair, and vomited. I kept her in a travelling basket overnight to prevent her falling and took her to the vet first thing in the morning.

She was suffering from vertigo caused by an injury to her eardrum, he explained. The only treatment was loving care to ensure she didn't fall into the fire or otherwise injure herself and wait for her to adapt. This she did over the next few weeks but for the remainder of her life her head tipped slightly to one side and a sudden fright or rough handling caused a recurrence of loss of balance. Already frail she was now fragile and no way could I consider sending her off to stud. I made the sad decision to have her spayed.

When I took her in for her operation, the vet took the unusual step of asking me to be at the surgery to collect her before she came round from the anaesthetic.

'There is such a special bond between you, I feel it will help her recover if she finds herself at home with you when she comes round.' He explained.

Less than a year later, I was dismayed when I felt a lump in her mammary glands. Back to the vet for another major operation, she came home with four stitches, a large wound on such a very small cat, and a warning to me; if the growth recurred it would not be wise to re-operate. The alternative did not bear thinking about, but a year later the lump was back.

At that time I was writing regular animal pieces for GLOBAL LIGHT Magazine, edited by Gordon Turner, a well-known Spiritual healer who treated both human and animal patients. In a last desperate bid to save my beloved little friend I appealed to him. He promised to include Tiny in his regular absent healing session.

When Gordon said, 'Let me know *when* it disappears.' not *if,* I allowed myself to hope. I knew what a wonderful man he was and how much he cared about animals yet I was amazed when it began to reduce in size as soon as he started absent healing. Two weeks to the day from my request I was able to tell him that it had gone completely. It never reappeared.

It seemed fitting that my first experience of spirit healing, even though I was familiar with the concept through Gordon's writing, should benefit my much loved little feline guru.

7

JUST THE TWO OF US

Perfect companions never have less
than four feet.

Colette

I accepted that Fate had knocked on the head my ambition to breed blue-eyed white cats when Tiny was spayed, but I still had my Brownies.

Tabitha and Tiberius (Tiny's tabby son) produced truly beautiful Brown tabby kittens, whole litters as alike as a bunch of bumble bees. As both parents were now full champions, these kittens were always in demand and often sold at birth or before. I could see no reason why this couldn't continue, then something totally unforeseen happened. Lovely and lovable sweet natured Tabitha declared war on Becky, my parent's Boxer, who had never shown anything but gentle kindness to the cats. Her loving concern when Tiny was so small and sick had given her warmth and comfort. Now Tabitha attacked her at every opportunity and no-one had any idea why, least of all Becky. If this happened today I would talk to the animals and try and find the reason for such aberrant behaviour.

Becky never retaliated, even when blood streamed down her face from deep scratches on her domed head. She could not be expected to stand this treatment indefinitely and if Becky was finally driven to retaliation it would bode ill for Tabitha. Something had to be done—but what?

An advertisement in the cat press, or even word of mouth in cat circles would almost certainly have meant I could sell her to a breeder, but she was so lovable, so zany, my friend, not an object with a commercial value. The solution came quite out of the blue. Someone who had one of her daughters as a dearly loved pet, phoned me to see if I had a companion for her; she jumped at the chance to give Tabitha a home. As soon as she recovered from her de-sexing operation she left for a new home in Gloucestershire. Parting with her was heart breaking but when I heard she and her daughter had been overjoyed to be reunited and she had settled well and was very much loved, I was happy for her.

It seemed the cat breeding phase of my life was over, I was to learn that it is not so easy to get rid of a bug as that, I had itchy feet and the wide world once again beckoned. My parents were happy to look after Tiberius, known to his friends as Timmy, and Gussie. She and my father enjoyed a special bond, he had such faith in her taste buds that he once took the cheese back to the grocer on the grounds that she didn't like it.

There was no question of leaving Tiny. I took a job on the outskirts of Oxford that had a small furnished flat going with it. Life was pleasant enough but a bit staid. I wanted to be more in the swim and believed I could earn enough as a free-lance journalist so I took a flat in Oxford and embarked on six months of lean living.

Tiny never complained in the hard times when cheques were few and small, often with long periods between, and rent had to paid regularly. She shared my diet of soup, baked beans and sardines, and spent hours watching for my return from an upstairs window when I was out. Something I only discovered when the occupant of the flat below mine told me that she always knew when I was coming home because she heard Tiny jump down from the window sill to meet me at the door. When shillings were in short supply for the gas meter we kept each other warm.

She must have been delighted when that chilly Winter and Spring came to an end, and I moved to London to share a flat with my sister and take up gainful employment once more. This was in reality a tiny house in Barnes, opposite the river. It was enchanting, one room wide but two stories high. The ground floor was half below ground, the cheerful royal blue front door reached by a flight of steps down from the pavement. This meant that the window of the large bed-sitting room was just above the top of the heads of people walking by on the pavement. Tiny loved to sit here on summer evenings watching the world go by and when footsteps paused, and a disembodied voice, usually female, exclaimed 'Oh—do look at that sweet little cat!' she drew herself up and turned into the room with a pleased smile, quite aware that she was being admired.

I would have loved to have stayed there, but we only had it for the summer while the owner was overseas. It even had a cat flap leading to a walled patio garden. Not quite perfect for although the wall kept Tiny in, it did not keep the neighbourhood cats out. None of them stayed however, it appeared to be a recognised shortcut for the feline inhabitants of the area. Tiny was incensed by their casual use of what she soon considered her domain but her cursing was ignored.

With the end of summer there was nothing for it but to move once more and I was lucky enough to find the perfect solution to finding living accommodation for us both and be able to write. I found a spacious top floor flat in a large house in St. John's Wood rent free in exchange for part time care of a two year old. With no rent to pay, meals when I was in charge of Mandy-Lou, who was a delightful child, I could make ends meet with my writing income. My employers were charming people who had no objection to Tiny sharing the flat with me. They loved animals and had two small dogs themselves. A small balcony opened off my kitchen and here Tiny was once more able to gaze out over London. We were both very happy and comfortable. Then out of the blue came a letter from Devon,

It was a request from the breeder who had bought Tiny's daughter, Candy, to take her back as a gift. When I enquired why she was so anxious to get rid of her I was told that the lady's husband insisted she go. She had bitten him, quite badly, and was threatening to do so again.

I expected to be told that one cat was all I could keep, but 'You must get her as quickly as possible,' I was instructed, 'before she is put down.' She echoed my own thoughts when she added 'The wretched man must have done something to her first.' Her owner lost no time getting her on a train for the long journey from Devon.

8

PRIDE COMES BEFORE A FALL

It is impossible to understand cats on the strength of superficial acquaintance.

Michael Joseph

There were no problems when the two cats met as both were overjoyed. They had parted three years before when Candy was only ten weeks old, but their pleasure in their reunion left me in no doubt they knew each other.

I, on the other hand, did not really know Candy at all. I had bred her and known her for the first ten weeks of her life but I knew nothing about the three years when she had lived in Devon, only that she had come back to me more or less in disgrace. Instead of finding out what traumatic experience had triggered her behaviour, I saw only the very beautiful cat she had become. Failing to see the poor cat's nerves were shot to pieces, I entered her in one of the London Shows and by the end of the day mine were not much better.

Down in the basement of the Show Hall I felt the first prickle of unease when I saw that the vet doing the ubiquitous health check on the entries was a man. When Candy realised that I was actually handing her to him she lost her cool completely and became a writhing panic stricken monster with twice the normal compliment of claws. The vet shrank back and made no attempt to take charge of her. I felt his behaviour was wussy as I sped after her. She made for the steps that led to wide open doors and London. The stream of arrivals descending with their calm, sensible well adjusted cats formed an advancing wall of human legs. Unable to read she made for what appeared to be another exit. It was the Men's toilets; desperation lent wings to my feet and length to my arm; I caught her in the entrance.

That was when I should have given up; instead I located a woman vet who very quickly cleared her. I settled her in her pen and left the hall.

I returned shortly after mid-day and hurried to her pen to inspect her Award cards. A dismal sight greeted me; not a single bright coloured card, just large black letters on a plain white card spelling out the words *'This Cat Could Not Be judged. She bites!'*

I felt deeply ashamed when she greeted me with obvious pleasure, how could I have been so insensitive as to inflict this on her? No-one was allowed to leave until the end of the day so we both had to endure the humiliation.

'Well ...' I thought 'pride really does come before a fall.' I lifted her from the cage and was holding her close, promising never to inflict a Show on her again, when a pleasant female voice behind me said, 'The lipstick on the top of her head rather belies that notice!' I turned round and smiled gratefully at the woman behind me. 'Such a pity'—she added—'she is so beautiful!'

I kept my promise and worked on improving my acquaintance with the real Candy, the cat inside the beautiful exterior.

What I found was a sweet, loving and gentle cat. Nervous of all strangers, panic stricken and paranoid if they were men. Few of my visitors caught a glimpse of her. I wondered what the bitten husband had done to cause this. If she heard so much as a creak outside my door she hid, usually under the cover of the divan in the bed-sitting room. Here she remained, a slight bump so seldom noticed that I sometimes had to warn people not to sit on her. Then one evening I brought in a new friend for coffee, my mouth was actually open to deliver this warning when Candy emerged, walked over to him and rubbed round his legs. He bent and stroked her, and didn't get bitten or even growled at. This behaviour was repeated every time he visited. What is more she didn't even hide when he was there.

I was impressed. Six months later we were married and the three of us, Tiny, Candy and I settled into a large farmhouse and a very different life for all of us than our London flat. They relished the freedom and space, the kitchen alone was almost the size of the entire flat and might have been designed with cats' comfort in mind with a huge sunny window ledge at one end and an Aga stove at the other. I often wonder if Candy secretly congratulated herself for bringing about this lifestyle change. She calmed down about strangers but my husband remained the only man she totally trusted.

There was a brief anxious moment when Tiny first met my father-in-law's feisty terrier with a reputation for chasing cats. He now lived in a cottage only a field away and on a visit to his old home met Tiny. We watched the confrontation anxiously; ready to rescue Tiny. It was not necessary, She stood her ground, staring him down for what seemed to us a very long time, then slowly, turning his head away, Pippin stepped off the path and walked round her. It was a remarkable demonstration of the power of the mind.

It was a chilly morning when John brought the visiting vet into the kitchen for coffee introducing him to me as Dr. Death. I wondered if he had made a genuine mistake or was 'taking the Mickey'. Tiny, waiting for a drink of warm milk when we had coffee and normally sociable with no fear of vets, stared at him in undisguised horror, and darted for cover under the furniture. He was definitely not amused by my comment that she hadn't liked the name. He fixed me with a stern eye and repeated several times that his name was pronounced De-Ath. I could see she didn't like him either. I respected her judgement and chose a different vet for my cats.

Tiny was brave, loving and extremely clever in human ways. She could do things like taking yeast tablets out of a jar with her paw. This skill earned her a year's supply of all that manufacturer's products for cats. I noticed that she invariably used her left paw and was intrigued when I read that the majority of cats are left pawed meaning that the right side of the brain was dominant leading researchers to the conclusion that cats are very intuitive. Tiny understood almost everything that was said to her and had the courage to face down strange and ferocious dogs ten times her size, but when it came to everyday cat skills she didn't seem to have any. Although a good and loving mother of three litters, she never knew how to pick up her kittens. The only thing she ever caught in her life was a large moth, she held it under her paw, looked up at me asking what to do with it then lifted her paw and released it, completely unharmed. Worst of all, when she climbed trees she could never get down and invariably had to be rescued.

She was my constant companion for ten years, through the tough times and the good. We were seldom separated. I loved her most dearly, admired her and respected her. She taught me so much about life, love and relationships as well as about cats. In spite of her frail physical body she was a cat of immense power. I could not imagine life without her.

Tiny's death was her final lesson for me She simply settled in her special bed by the stove and died purring. She looked comfortable, relaxed and at peace. She was not sick, or suffering in any way; yet I knew with complete certainty she was preparing to leave me. It was a mellow afternoon in early autumn, there were just the two of us in a stillness that had an air of sanctity about it. I picked her up and held her gently in my arms looking down into the beloved face with its strange odd eyes. Tears welled; for a moment I could not bear it, then through the sound of her purr I heard the voice in my head; she was saying 'goodbye' The thought of going on without her was bleak. But her words made it clear the time had come for us to part.

'You are all right now; you don't need me any more, I can go.'

I knew in my heart she spoke the truth. I loved her as much as ever and I should miss her dreadfully; but I no longer needed her in the same way now I had a husband and a young son. I held her close for a few precious moments and let the tears fall. Then I thanked her for all she had given to me, gave her my blessing and told her it was all right for her to leave. I laid her gently back in her bed and within a few minutes her spirit left her body. She was only ten years old.

We buried her with love and reverence in her favourite place in the garden. How strange, I thought, that after all her life-threatening illnesses she was in perfect health when she died.

Caroline Myss, in her book *Anatomy Of The Spirit*, says that souls who have attained a certain level of spiritual consciousness can die when they feel the time is right. She cites as examples the Buddha and the great spiritual teacher Sogyal Rinpoche, author of *The Tibetan Book Of Living And Dying*. I believe Tiny had reached that level and was indeed a great soul.

Her death made me question our attitude to animals and the role they play in our lives. At worst we see them as possessions; ours to use as we wish. At best we think of ourselves as their guardians and caretakers, but still with power, albeit God like. Maybe in our arrogance we have got it wrong; these seemingly helpless inferior beings are special souls who choose to share our lives as our guides and mentors, our guardian angels?

I am by no means the only person to have their life affected and directed by a white cat. Cleveland Amory, well known American author and humanitarian and founder of the

Fund For Animals, rescued an injured white cat on Christmas Eve 1977. He was so filthy he didn't realise he was white until he bathed him. He called him Polar Bear and wrote a book; *THE CAT WHO CAME FOR CHRISTMAS* which was published in fifteen different countries and became an international best seller. Their friendship lasted fourteen years and when Polar died he was buried at one of the refuges established by The Fund For Animals. The memorial over his grave reads *"Beneath these stones lie the mortal remains of The Cat Who Came For Christmas, Beloved Polar Bear, "Till we meet again."*

Seven years later Cleveland Amory himself died and was laid to rest beside his feline friend.

9

SWEET AS HONEY

Sphinx of my quiet hearth … friend of my toil,
companion of mine ease, thine is
the lore of Ra and Ramses.

Rosamond Marriott Watson

I took Candy to be mated to a magnificent aristocratic white long haired cat before leaving London; she had six beautiful kittens. They appeared strong and healthy at birth yet one after the other they faded away. This was heartbreaking for both Candy and I for her mothering was exemplary. This should have killed my enthusiasm for breeding cats, alas it only convinced me I was not meant to breed white cats.

Once spayed Candy settled down very happily to country life and the freedom of a large house and garden. I am sure she was relieved when I told her there would be no more Shows, from now on she could just enjoy being a cat.

Life was busy and enjoyable, I had my two much loved white cats for feline company; breeding and showing cats was just one of those things I used to do, wasn't it?

My son was eight months old when I succumbed to temptation—yet again; I bought an eight week old Abyssinian kitten with the express intention of making a comeback to the world of pedigree cats.

I had always admired the tawny coats and lithe sinuous appearance of these jungle creatures in miniature which, according to Sidney Denham, author of the book *CHILD OF THE GODS* were almost identical in appearance to the sacred cat of the Ancient Egyptians; and thus the most domesticated of all cats. They may have a look of the wild but several thousand years of domestication, adoration and worship helped to create a personality described by Sidney Denham as '*...having a particularly sweet nature, great intelligence and a sense of humour plus a great desire for the company of humans.*' My kitten displayed all these character traits in spite of looking like a miniature lynx. There was nothing in the least wild about her nature; the name given to her by my husband when I released her from her travelling basket suited her perfectly. Her registered pedigree name was Shybu Aurum but when he said 'She is rather a honey isn't she?' Honey she became.

She and my baby son were delighted with each other. The species barrier dissolved when these two babies met in favour of youth. They spent most of their waking hours together and some sleep time too. Neither was ever hurt in the slightest.

Our Victorian farmhouse had a staircase from the tiled hall to a large landing beneath a cathedral ceiling. This was where Honey loved playing 'fetch'. She raided the trash bin in my study for a suitable ball of waste paper and dropped it at my feet for me to throw down into the hall. She tore after it, taking a shortcut through the banisters, grabbed the paper in her teeth, skidded across the tiles to the foot of the stairs, up the flight incredibly fast, dropped the paper at my feet and waited for me to throw it again. All at such high speed that I barely had time to catch my breath between throws.

All three cats loved the large kitchen; it was the hub of the house. As well as the Aga and the sunny window sill there were comfortable chairs and the playpen. The bars of this were no barrier to Honey who often joined my son inside. If she was tired she could snooze in the sun among the pot plants and if she felt wicked shin up the curtains and grin down at me, well aware that I could not reach her.

'Helping me cook' i.e. Licking out bowls was on the top of her list of favourite things to do. The role of assistant cook naturally involved tasting things. I had only to blink and she was dipping a slim paw into my cake mix and licking it thoughtfully. Unabashed by my protests she merely commented 'I think it

65

needs a little more egg.'

I was prepared to forgive her sampling the raw mixture, the heat of the oven would kill any germs, but I was furious the day I left a perfectly rolled Swiss roll cooling, and Honey apparently asleep, to answer the phone. I returned to find her, very much awake, consuming warm Swiss roll at incredible speed. To compound the felony she had eaten from both ends. My curses fell on deaf ears, Honey was too busy washing Swiss Roll crumbs from her whiskers.

I gave the cats beaten raw egg as a treat when my hens obliged by laying well. Honey could hear a fork touching the side of a bowl from anywhere in the house or garden; when she nicked out into the garden on the crisp winter dawn of her first show a fork banging round an empty bowl brought her in at high speed to be bundled into her travelling container; we caught the early morning train by a whisker.

Every now and then when she was being especially outrageous or sparkly I allowed myself to wonder if maybe, just maybe, Tabitha was back in another body. Honey, too, loved an audience as I discovered when I opened the door to a young man who had come to see my husband hoping to sell him some piece of farm equipment. I explained that he was out but he insisted on giving me his prepared spiel. I wished he would just give me the pamphlets

66

he shook now and then to emphasise his words and go. Then he stopped in mid-sentence, his eyes focused beyond me. Honey was strolling towards the door, exaggerating, I was sure, the elegant swaying walk that the long hind legs of her breed gave her. The eyes of the would-be salesman followed her languid progress as she sauntered past and sat down on the path near him. He turned to me with the bemused expression of someone who has fallen suddenly, and irrevocably in love.

'What a glorious cat …' he sighed 'that walk—exactly like a mannequin.' Another love-lorn sigh, 'What sort is she?'

'An Abyssinian.' I told him, thrown by this abrupt departure from his well-rehearsed sales patter. He whipped out a Biro from his pocket, repeated the word and wrote it down on the pamphlets still in his hand, thanked me very much and departed, still clutching them.

I never knew what he was trying to sell and never saw him again; I hope he found an Abyssinian cat.

'You show-off.' I told Honey; she gave me a smug little cat smile.

I bought her a smart gold cat harness to tone with her coat and match her eyes and without any teaching she walked with grace wherever I led her. I had succumbed once more to the fascinating world of cat shows. Living within easy reach of London I could get there and back in a day. I put her harness on before she got in her travelling box and when we were ensconced, usually the only occupants, in a first class compartment, I clipped her lead on and let her out. She got immense enjoyment from sitting on my lap with her front paws on the window ledge so that she could watch the world rushing past the window. If I heard the ticket collector coming I tried to get her in her box, but even the sternest one, who informed me that I should have a ticket for her but didn't insist, fell for her charm.

There were eight bedrooms in the farmhouse, one of which was very large and very empty. It made an ideal kitten nursery. It was also directly above my husband's office. He was closeted with his accountant when Honey's four lively kittens were about seven weeks old. They made an incredible and rather strange noise pounding about overhead on the polished floorboards chasing each other and their ping-pong ball. My husband was amused when his visitor after glancing at the ceiling several times finally lost the thread of the conversation, cleared his throat and asked— 'Err—do you have a mouse problem—or even rats?'

Honey shared our home and our life for five years, loved and admired by all who knew her when our lives and therefore those of our much-loved animals were drastically disrupted. My father in law died and my husband inherited the farm and an overwhelming burden in the form of death duties. After much agonising we decided to sell up and start afresh on the other side of the world.

If I could travel back in time I doubt if I would do it again; the heartbreak and anguish parting with our large and much loved animal family was too great. We had dogs, ponies, a donkey and of course my beloved cats. Not only those who lived with us in the house but the small family of cats who lived in the extensive barns. I found homes for all, and can only hope they were good ones.

I can still feel the grief and the guilt that wracked me watching Honey's enjoyment of her last train ride. I felt I was betraying her trust in me. It was only now, with the moment of parting drawing near, that I realised how much I valued her, not for her commercial value but for her enchanting personality.

At Paddington station I handed her over to the breeder of Abyssinian cats who had bought her. When she told me that all her cats lived in a cattery I wanted to snatch her back, Honey had always had complete freedom and been a member of the family. Travelling back on the train I choked back the tears; I knew I had made a terribly wrong decision, a knowledge that was to haunt me for many years.

I finally accepted that breeding cats was just not on. I had thought that having a pedigree made them secure, in this instance it had the reverse effect, because my darling Abyssinian had a commercial value it had indeed been easy to place her in a new home; yet, had I had the wit to see into the future that very commercial value would have made it viable to take her with us to Australia.

Taking cats to Australia was almost as costly as taking children. I was already taking Tilly, a plain black and white cat with a limp who I thought, no one would want, and with whom I had a very special and close relationship. She had already been delivered to the shippers in Cambridge. I never regretted taking her but I did wish, many, many times that I had taken Honey as well whatever the cost. When I discovered that one of the finest Abyssinian stud cats in South-eastern Australia lived in Tasmania, the island state that was our destination, the knife turned in my heart; Honey would have added to the gene pool of Abyssinian cats in Australia and her kittens would have been eagerly sought after.

As I opened up more to the idea of cats sharing more than one life with human souls they have grown to love, I became more convinced that my funny, loving intelligent little Abyssinian friend was on a return trip. It added to my feeling of guilt that I had let her down.

Honey was undeniably special and physically like the cats of Ancient Egypt but I don't think this was because she was a pure bred Abyssinian cat. Every cat is a unique individual and in every one there is more than a little of the goddess. I look into the eyes of my feline friends today and see reflected there the memory of three thousand years of being worshipped as divine and feel I am being asked to remember it too.

10

TILLY—THE TRAVELLER

*Felines are dream walkers
—they straddle the worlds.*
Amelia Kinkade

'I want this one?' I held in my hand a small black and white kitten; my first meeting with a very special cat. My friend, who was giving me first pick of a litter of three kittens born to her warehouse cat, and I would both have laughed aloud if someone had told us that this rather ordinary scrap of cat was destined to cross the world.

The mother cat lived in a grocery warehouse, which she kept free of vermin. A kitten from her I reasoned would not know about houses and would be quite happy to live in our extensive granaries to augment the vermin control staff already there and which had, over the last year or so become seriously depleted in numbers. These cats, inherited from my mother-in-law, were not like so many farm cats I have known, semi-wild and poorly fed. They were tame and enjoyed one good meal every day fed to them in the loft closest to the house. The farm buildings were a distance away from the house and none had ever attempted to become house cats, or even been seen away from the farm buildings. A kitten born of a renowned hunting mother in a warehouse seemed a perfect addition.

There were three kittens in the litter, two handsome tabby and white males, replica's of their mother, and this black and white female. I had no hesitation in choosing her. I wondered afterwards if it was her likeness to long dead Mrs Muggins that influenced my choice. With the wisdom of hindsight I could see that it would have suited my purpose much better to choose the two males.

'Are you sure you want that one?' Even as my friend asked the question I saw she was pleased. 'I didn't think anyone would want her...' she added. 'But I did promise you first pick.'

I said I was quite sure and happily bore my eight-week-old kitten home and ensconced her in the barn where the cats lived without taking her anywhere near the house.

I left her exploring and introducing herself to the cats in residence and walked back to the house. This took several minutes, as I had to cross a small paddock, past the garages and across the top of the wide drive. It entailed opening and closing two gates. I walked quickly, glancing over my shoulder several times to check she was not following.

I entered the house at the nearest point, through a side door and followed the long passage to the kitchen. In this solid Victorian house doors were thick, keeping sound in, or out, and reducing it considerably from one part of the house to another. After one last glance over my shoulder I closed the doors behind me. It would soon be time for afternoon tea so I moved the kettle over to the hot spot on the Aga and paused, my hand still on the handle. Surely I was imagining the piercing screams of an outraged kitten?

I retraced my steps to the outside door and faced a tiny black and white figure, bristling with indignation. I returned her to the place where I intended her to live. By the time I had done this five times the day had moved forward and it was definitely afternoon teatime. I was ready to give up.

'I thought she was supposed to be a farm cat. You'll never get her to live in the granary if you bring her into the house.' My husband, in for a cup of tea, looked down at Tilly. I had given her a name on the way home, sitting, with the satisfied composure of one who has triumphed over great odds, in front of the Aga.

'I did not bring her. I took her straight to the granary, she brought herself.' I gritted at this injustice and with my back to them both poured boiling water into the teapot.

'I'll take her back and get away quickly so she won't see me go.' He told me smugly as he swept her up and marched to the door.

'She doesn't have to see you—she knows the way.' But I was talking to his back.

'You just have to be quick.' He told me confidently as he came back and sat down at the kitchen table.

Silently I poured the tea, passed a cup over to him and waited. Not for long, his hand raising the cup to his lips stopped mid-way as piercing, and very indignant shrieks were heard.

'Is that her?' He stared at me, put down his untouched tea, pushed his chair back then determination in every line, marched to the door.

By the time he had done this several times and the shrieks were rather hoarse but had lost none of their indignation and determination, he gulped down his now cool tea walked to the door and let her in. She bounced into the kitchen ahead of him. 'I think,' he admitted ruefully, 'that we have to admit she has won.'

I agreed 'I am afraid she has.' Bowing to the inevitable I poured her a saucer of milk. Working so hard to get your own way was thirsty work

We smiled as she finally turned towards us, a large pearl of milk on her chin, and gave us a small pink mew of gratitude, or was it triumph?

What incredible determination we agreed, and wondered how an eight week old kitten, born in a warehouse who, until today, had never left it, to a mother who herself had never been a house cat, had known about houses and that some cats lived good lives in them? Was it some mystic inborn knowing or had her mother instructed her to set the rules for her future life immediately. Having chosen to be a house cat she never went near the farm buildings again.

We soon realised that we had adopted an extraordinary cat. We didn't know then that she was destined to live a life that, by normal cat standards, would also be extraordinary. By the time she died at the early age of eight, she had experienced incredible adventures, lost a few lives along the way and earned the love and admiration of the entire family. Sometimes when I looked at her little black and white person I remembered Muggins and wondered.

11

THE HAND OF FATE

If you are worthy of its affection a cat will be your friend but never your slave

Theophile Gautier

A knock at the back door disturbed us at breakfast. Tilly was now about a year old. A young man held out what appeared to be a dead cat. Behind him a young woman sobbed noisily.

'I didn't hit her...' he said hastily, 'we saw her come out of your drive and get hit by the car in front of us. We stopped and picked her up, even though she was dead we thought you would want to know what had happened to her.'

As I murmured my thanks for his kindness she sprang dramatically to life, leapt to the ground and vanished in the lush summer garden.

I found her in the raspberry canes, dazed, but washing. A small patch of blood on the flap of one ear was the extent of her injuries.

Her next brush with death a year later was much more serious and changed the direction of her life. It led to her migrating to Australia.

I was sitting outside on the garden seat shelling peas on a hot Sunday morning in mid-summer when my neighbour turned in the drive gate. Unlike me she was dressed in her Sunday best.

'I ran over one of your cats on my way to church...' she began without any preamble. 'Don't worry it wasn't your Abyssinian, or I would have stopped on my way; but I was running late and she was dead anyway so I kept going. . .' Her voice trailed away before she took another breath and continued; 'It's a black and white one—one of your farm cats I suppose; but I thought I had better let you know.'

'Where is she?' I found a croaky voice.

'On the grass verge, near your drive gate.' It dawned on her I was not taking this news lightly; certainly not with gratitude that she had informed me. As she drove out of the gate my husband, carrying a spade he had been working in the vegetable garden, appeared with our five-year-old son.

'Was she saying that she ran over her on her way to church and told you on her way back?'

I nodded, 'Yes—she seemed to think I should be grateful it wasn't Honey.'

'Some religion—I'll get her...' the words *and bury her* hung in the air between us.

'Mummy—she's not dead! Daddy says she is breathing and her heart is beating.' He was running ahead of my husband who was bearing the spade held carefully horizontal in front of him with the small still form lying on it. He had scooped her up carefully to avoid adding to her injuries.

'Put her in the back of the station wagon ...' I suggested, 'she'll be safe there and I'll take her straight to the vet.' Then I remembered it was Sunday, his clinic would not be open. I hurried indoors and called his home number.

My heart dropped when his wife told me he was out on a call. 'But he is at a farm quite near you. I'll see if I can catch him and send him straight on to you.'

When the vet arrived, (not Dr. Death, I had taken my cats to a different one after Tiny's reaction) he examined her thoroughly, expertly and very gently; she was by now beginning to show a few signs of life.

'She's badly concussed, her right hip has suffered some damage, and she has extensive bruising; but I can't find any broken bones.' He told me. I ground my teeth when he added, 'Lying in the sun for so long has not helped.'

An anxious childish treble asked the question I dare not 'Will she die?'

'If she were a dog—or a human—she would be dead now ...' I felt a shard of hope at the vet's words as he added 'but as she is a cat I would say she has a fifty/fifty chance.'

'Shall you take her back to your hospital?' I wanted to know.

He shook his head. 'If anything kills her it

78

will be shock. If you can keep her immobile so that her damaged hip has a chance to mend she will be better at home. In her own surroundings with the people she loves her chances could rise to sixty/forty. In the atmosphere of my animal hospital she would probably just give up and die. She will always have a limp and will almost certainly abort her kittens, but keep her as immobile as possible for a couple of weeks with plenty of fluids and as much nourishing food as she will eat; but above all let her know you care.'

A friend who bred miniature dachshunds offered the loan of a crate; we transferred her carefully to it and installed her in the quietest room in the house. She did, as predicted, lose the kittens. I followed his advice especially about assuring her of my love for her and amazingly a couple of weeks later she was limping round the house.

That she had been left at the side of the road that fateful day because she was just an ordinary cat made me question once again the ethics of breeding pedigree cats. All life was precious, An ordinary 'moggie' felt no less pain than an aristocratic cat.

The bond between us was now so strong that I knew I could not leave her behind when we left for Australia. After all who would want a plain little black and white cat with a permanent limp?

She still had a pronounced limp when we

took her to Cambridge and saw her installed in the little kennel built like a motel room for cats. It had a little sleeping compartment and a small wire run. A drawer that just had to be pulled out supplied her toilet. She would live in this for four weeks then be transferred to a quarantine kennels in Melbourne for a further two months. Would I ever see my dear little friend again and if I did would she remember me, or would the traumatic experience of crossing the world and being imprisoned in quarantine make her forget her family and her previous life?

The rain was coming down in relentless straight lines, as I climbed to the top deck of The Princess of Tasmania; I was tense with a mixture of anticipation and anxiety.

'How will I know where she is' I asked as I surveyed the long line of little boxes. My answer was swift, a piercing shriek from the far end, 'I'm here!'

How could I imagine for a second that she would forget me, any more than I could her?

Her paws went round my neck, her face rubbed against my cheek; as the loudest purr ever heard thrummed in my ear. I held her close for a few moments before putting her securely in the travelling box.

Safe in the car I let her out and she moved from one member of the family to another with little squeaks and prrts of joy, every now and then looking out of the window at the new world passing before her.

As we started on the hour-long journey the sun came out, it was already shining inside the car. With her arrival the strange house in a new country became home.

I gave her twenty-four hours inside the house to get her bearings, she looked out of every window in turn imprinting on her mind a map of what was out there. The next day I let her go where and when she wanted. She was delighted to find that there were hay barns with mice in them and rabbits in the paddocks and settled down immediately, as happy to be back with us as we all were to have her. The enforced rest at sea and in quarantine had worked a miracle; she no longer had any trace of a limp and was fit and sleek.

I am ashamed to admit that she was never de-sexed, I am not quite sure why except that I had not grasped the vital importance of de-sexing. The only way cats will be valued is if they are in short supply. Fortunately she was not very prolific, two kittens or for the most three were all she ever had at a time. She fraternised happily with the locals and it was not long before we had a cat family again and many of our new friends had half English kittens.

When she disappeared for two days I was desperate. I thought it unlikely she had been run over again for we lived up a long steep lane well off the road. Snake bite was my big fear. Then she limped in with a grossly swollen front paw and I knew she had been caught in a rabbit snare. Fortunately whoever was responsible for setting it had released her. She spent most of the next two weeks indoors, healing.

Four years after our arrival in Tasmania we moved again, this time across the Bass Strait to Victoria.

By this time we had our entire donkey stud, ten stud cattle, three cats, a pet sheep and a dog. All these were to travel in a large truck, they would be driven to the docks at Burnie and the semi trailer would be loaded onto the boat. The prime mover would then return to its base in Launceston and another driver would meet the boat at Melbourne and take the semi to our new property in Central Victoria. My husband was to drive the car and the horse float, both loaded with everything we could cram in, our furniture would go in a furniture removal van on the same boat and the three children and I would fly over and be at the new house to greet all this when it arrived after the overnight crossing. We had to fly out from Devonport but the boat went from Burnie. A friend from Devonport very kindly volunteered to ferry me and the children to the Airport. A perfectly planned operation, till Tilly added her unique touch.

She chose not to come in the night before departure day. No doubt deciding to have a last hunt in what she considered a very pleasant place. When she didn't turn up for breakfast I was frantic. We all called and searched, the truck arrived and loaded up all the other animals, they left for the docks followed by the loaded car and the horse-float. Only the children and I remained on the empty property to await our friends from Devonport. We spent the time searching for Tilly. I rang my next-door neighbour who lived at the bottom of our hill. She promised me she would care for her when she turned up, and send her by plane to Melbourne.

The car arrived and after one last desperate call we all climbed in. The children protested that we couldn't go without Tilly. We were all close to tears. As the car turned to head back down the lane there was a united cry of 'Stop!'

Through my blurred vision I could see that the small black and white figure trotting towards the car was yelling 'Hey—wait for me!'

I leapt out and snatched her up in my arms. The friends who had so kindly offered to take us to the airport had not bargained for the frantic race along the coast road to Burnie where I was just in time to bundle Tilly in with the other cats before everything was loaded onto the ferry then another wild dash back along the coast and on to Devonport where by some miracle we managed to catch our flight to Melbourne.

That night as I relaxed at last in the Motel, I sent my thoughts winging to my little friend somewhere out on the Bass Strait. Was it coincidence that she turned up at the crucial moment? Maybe, but I could not believe that she had not heard us calling and seen the departure of our home and the other animals. This, I decided, was Cat Power. She was confident she would not be abandoned and such was the bond between us she probably also knew that, like her, I loved our Tasmanian home and did not want to leave.

When we met up next day she was completely unfazed and settled immediately into the new home. For two years she continued to fill our house and our lives with love and happiness and added a few more Anglo-Australian cats to the family. I sometimes felt she treated her nine lives with a somewhat casual abandon and was always anxious when she was missing for longer than usual, but she was a free spirit and lived her life so fully that I could scarcely believe that she was only eight years old when she staggered into the kitchen one Saturday morning, mewed piteously and collapsed on the floor. Within about fifteen minutes she was dead.

We were all devastated; loving and lovable, often funny, sometimes exasperating, she was family. My children could not recall life without her.

She had lived an extraordinarily adventurous life by cat standards; and she had lived it with courage and gusto, but now her nine lives had run out. She had spanned two worlds in every sense; I never doubted her vibrant spirit lived on in some other dimension but even though I had always told her that if ever another cat came into my life with the aggravating habit of banging her head against my hand when I was pouring milk I would know she had come back, I did not consciously wait for her return.

It was many years later that I was to remember how often I had said this when a black and white cat who was almost her double thanked me for the first drink of milk I ever gave her by knocking it all over the floor in just the same way.

Tilly taught me the truth of the maxim; *It is not what happens to you in life—but how you take it*. I have always cherished the memory of the small kitten, snatched from her mother and everything familiar, deciding that the life of a barn cat was not for her and by sheer strength of will creating an amazing future for herself. This was power indeed.

12

CAT CHAT

*My cat does not talk as respectfully to me
as I do to her.*

Colette

I closed my book, placed it on the bedside
table with a slight sigh of relief. The sound of a
car followed by the front door closing told me
my teenage daughter was safely home.

A few moments later my smile of greeting
turned to questioning astonishment when
I met the large round eyes of the black and
white cat staring back at me from her arms.
A charge flowed between us in that brief
second of meeting, was it recognition or
acknowledgement that I was meeting the
guru who would teach me that meaningful
communication with animals, whether their
spirits were still in earthly bodies or had left
them to cross The Rainbow Bridge was a
reality?

I was aware of two pairs of eyes, the human
ones defensive and defiant, and the feline ones
challenging and definitely defiant. Neither my
daughter nor the cat had cause for concern
for it never for an instant crossed my mind to

say she could not stay, even though as usual, we had a large feline family. The cat and I continued to stare at each other as I waited to hear her story.

'She was at MacDonald's; the usual stray cats rummaging round their garbage bins late at night—I always speak to them' (of course) 'but none of them ever respond—they just vanish into the night. Not this one, She turned round and came straight to me. She wasn't in the least scared, but seemed rather cross—I felt she was saying; *Thank goodness you've come at last. What kept you?* So I put her in the car and brought her home.'

The cat and I continued to stare at one another; I looked into the large golden eyes and didn't doubt for a minute that my daughter's explanation was accurate.

'We'll call her Matilda.' I spoke the name without conscious thought. It was as if beloved English Tilly, who had now been dead for ten years, was there in front of me 'We will settle her in the kitchen.' I pushed my feet into slippers, reached for my robe and followed my daughter, the cat still in her arms, to the warmth of the wood burning range.

'I think she would like a drink of milk; she must be hungry—she was rummaging round the garbage bins when I saw her.'

Still under the hypnotic effect of those huge eyes looking directly into mine I reached for a cat dish, half filled it with fresh milk from our

Jersey cow, added hot water from the kettle simmering on the hob and reached down to place it in front of the cat.

As I did so a hard round head knocked my hand causing at least half the milk to spill on the floor; I clicked my tongue in exasperation then heard my own voice echoing down the years *'If ever another cat comes into my life and thanks me in this way I shall know it is you back.'*

We stared at one another, the cat who was now Matilda, and I; she seemed to be smiling and I know I was. *'Here I am,'* her smile said. I poured more milk, mopped up the floor and watched her finish her drink and settle in front of the wood stove to deal with her toilet. Her purr filled my heart as well as my ears as I closed the door and returned to bed.

She got up with a polite greeting as soon as I appeared next morning. I didn't need to enquire if she had slept well; her mien was calm and settled, not at all what one would expect of a cat in a strange place. I offered breakfast, which was graciously accepted. She did not cause any spills, then or ever again, there was no need, the point had been made. In the early morning bustle of a family nothing was done to keep her, doors were left open and she was free to come and go as she wished. The other cats and the dogs all accepted her as family, and she them. It was obvious to everyone that she was here to stay.

She became my mentor, my friend and my teacher; from her I learned valuable lessons about animal communication.

All my life I have been deeply interested in communication between humans and animals and between animals of different species who do not share the same vocal or body language yet understand each other. Dogs and cats are an obvious example of this. Careful observation and my own experience convinced me they were also using a form of telepathy or direct mind to mind communication.

My father always knew how animals felt and what they were thinking and I can remember being admonished for saying something unkind about our family dog because I would 'hurt his feelings'.

My own most vivid memory of receiving a message from an animal was when a horse instructed me to duck before it jumped over me; that I obeyed without question probably saved my life. My interest in inter-species communication had led to my researching the subject and writing a book on it. But I was not confident in my own ability to talk with animals, part of my mind suggesting that the messages I got had their genesis in my imagination. Matilda was the practical teacher I needed. She taught me that very real communication could, and did exist between living beings, whatever the species, and that it could continue after the death of the body.

We all hear animal lovers claiming that their beloved cat or dog understands every word they say. I didn't think they actually understood the words but picked up the image in the person's mind as they spoke them. I have revised this opinion; I now know there are many animals who do understand a great deal of what we actually say. But if we think one thing and say another our thoughts will take precedence over our words. We can see examples of this in training, if the human gives an order but in their heart does not believe the animal can, or will do it then the chances are it won't.

It is obvious that in dealing with animals we need to be scrupulously honest, saying the words out loud helps to clarify them in the mind; if mental telepathy is the key it will be easier for the animal to pick up the message. I do not think it is the only factor, just part of it, in the same way it can help understanding between us and other humans

There seemed to be an open channel between Matilda and I, she would think *Milk* and I would find myself going to the fridge. I discovered it worked the other way, if I could clear my mind sufficiently and then put a thought in it for her to do something simple, jump on the sofa and sit by me, for instance, she apparently got the message. I became quite excited about this and when she and I were together in a room I sent her a stream of messages, such as *'turn round and look at me'* . After enduring this for a while she decided to put a stop to such nonsense.

We were in the lounge together, I practising this skill on her, when she sat down firmly with her back to me. I put all my concentration on sending a message to Matilda's unresponsive back. I was brought up short by a testy little voice in my head.

'Shut up!' It was startlingly clear but I just went on staring at the little figure on the other side of the hearth. Then it was there again; 'I don't want to talk.'

I was momentarily stunned by the force and clarity of the words but I got the message, both immediately and in the wider sense. I didn't talk to her merely for practice any more, I politely asked her out loud if she would like to talk and never insulted her with stupid commands again.

This experience, which was so totally unexpected, taught me more about communicating with animals than any of the books I had read. I looked at Matilda with new respect.

How unnecessary to subject her to these tedious mind games. I knew that communication with animals was a reality; I had, I realised been doing it all my life to a lesser or greater degree. My wide reading told me it was a universal gift that anyone with a genuine love of animals and a real desire to learn, coupled with that valuable attribute, an open mind, could develop. Many of the messages I had received in the past, such as the one from the horse, had come in instantaneous flashes when least expected. I came to the conclusion that the key to successful communication was relaxation rather than concentration. Stilling the mind and going into that place where you and your animal friend can meet.

Shortly after I came to this realisation I faced my biggest challenge to prove that the communication between species I had so confidently written about was fact not fantasy.

Chloe, the youngest member of our cat family, was missing. For two days we called and searched, when I stood outside in the silence I was sure I heard a small desperate cat wail in the distance. I called and listened—and listened again. I looked up, something we had all failed to do, high above me, at the top of a very large gum tree saw a tiny black figure balanced precariously on a very thin branch.

I pointed her out to the family; we all stared up. In the silence we could hear a thin little miaow and by straining our eyes detect a pink mouth opening.

My husband got our longest ladder and bravely climbed it. He was still nowhere near her.

We discussed the possibility of hiring a cherry picker; 'Why don't *you* do something?'

my daughter demanded of me.

'I can't climb that ladder.' I protested, 'I'm no good at all on heights.'

'You could talk her down.'

'Talk her down?' I repeated blankly.

'Yes, you write enough and talk enough about communicating with animals, let's see you do it!' The entire family were looking at me—waiting. I looked up at Chloe desperately calling for help. I took a deep breath and bit the bullet.

'Go inside and leave me to it then.'

Left alone I circled the tree taking stock of Chloe's position. My heart sank, the branches in front of her, looked perilously thin, little more than twigs. If she stepped on any of them she would almost certainly fall. She needed to turn round to stronger branches. I took another deep breath, closed my eyes for a second and let Chloe and her predicament fill my senses. When I looked up again she was staring down at me. I knew she trusted me.

'Chloe...' I spoke her name to be sure I had her full attention then projected my consciousness into her so that I saw the tree from her perspective. Holding a picture in my mind of the branches surrounding her I told her in a clear voice exactly what she must do.

'Turn round...' I told her 'very carefully.' She did and was now facing stronger branches. Keeping quite still she waited for guidance. I studied the tree carefully before telling her where to move next, pointing as I did so. She followed my directions, moving carefully to the next branch. When she was just above my head she slithered the last bit down the trunk into my arms. She rubbed her cheek against mine, her ecstatic purr punctuated by little squeaks. I held her close, hardly able to believe it myself before carrying her into the house to enjoy my moment of triumph.

13

MATILDA—THE STORY OF A FRIENDSHIP

Jellicle cats are black and white………
Jellicle cats are merry and bright.

T.S. Elliott.

I enjoyed twelve years of companionship with Matilda, an enchanting, lovable, loving and clever cat who could also be very funny at times. A true 'Jellicle cat'.

I sometimes thought she had studied *The Silent Miaow* which does not have his name as the author but the words, *Translated From The Feline* by Paul Gallico on the title page.

Paul Gallico started his working life as a

sports journalist but went on to write some of the most exquisite books in the English language, many about animals and a great many about cats whom he loved and admired. He had a great insight into the feline psyche. The sub title of *The Silent Miaow* is *A manual for kittens, strays and homeless cats.* It tells cats how to take over a household and run it to his/ her liking.

'You may amuse them, (humans) so that they laugh with you but never at you' is one gem of advice followed by Matilda.

Cats have a highly developed sense of fun, many, like Matilda, a real sense of humour. She made me laugh frequently, but always sharing a joke with her, not at her expense.

Sitting on fences observing was one of her favourite pastimes. Shortly after she came to live with us the shearer came to give our two pet sheep their annual trim. We put them in a temporary holding pen on the paddock side of the garden post and rails. Here I found Matilda, front feet on the top, hind feet on the rail below, inches away from their woolly bodies peering in astonishment. She turned round and looked at me, her eyes two amazed question marks. 'What...' she asked; 'are these creatures? I never saw anything like them at Macdonalds.'

'Sheep.' I told her. You don't usually see them in town.'

She stared a few moments longer, then

95

climbed down and walked across the lawn towards me expressing her opinion of the strange creatures out loud.

She was not above enjoying another cat's discomfiture, especially when that cat was Dana who persistently teased her and tried to boss her. We had moved to a suburban house with a tall wooden fence separating us from the next-door property. Three cats lived here and to give them their due never came over the fence into our garden. Matilda liked to sit at the top of this fence on one of the uprights with her arms resting on top where she could safely watch the goings on next door. She was occupying her grandstand seat, when loud cat shrieks rent the air. She turned round and looked at me, her eyes glinting with glee, the message was clear;

'Just come and look at this—she's really getting it!'

I walked to the fence and peered over on tiptoe, Dana had ventured next door and the three cats who lived there were in a semicircle round her telling her in no uncertain tones to leave. She came back over that fence with a great deal of speed and very little dignity. Matilda's smile was smug; for once she had come off top cat.

Dana, found as a very small kitten outside the railway station, never treated her with the respect due to a more senior member of the household. Wrested from her natural mother too young, she was not always sure of the appropriate way for a cat to behave.

Matilda was a wonderful companion; so often just there when I was gardening or doing some other chore. She always sat as close as she could get without interfering. I could see she thought gardening a very odd pastime, I didn't seem to actually use any holes I dug. I was weeding the rockery, my mind thinking about a radical move I was considering, as if she picked up my thoughts Matilda moved closer and with a soft trill of affection rubbed her head against my gloved hand. It was unusual for her to actually make physical contact when I was working in the garden so I sat back on my heels and looked at her. In that instant I changed my mind, there was no way I could take any path in life that parted me from this loving and lovable cat. I smiled at her and wondered, is this my pet or my guardian angel?

She loved to lick the detachable beaters from my electric hand beater and did this with remarkable skill; she could turn them over and hold them up off the floor with her paw so that not a single drop of beaten egg, cream or cake mix was missed. She had a passion for ice cream and yoghurt, a treat she had no doubt first discovered rummaging among the garbage outside MacDonald's. I have often thought how odd it is that cats, who are so intelligent, do not seem to grasp the idea of putting their foot on something to stop it sliding about the floor when they lick it as many dogs do. Matilda was the exception; always keeping an ice cream carton or lid still with her paw as she enjoyed the treat.

Cats are renowned for their remarkable hearing. We admire them for their night vision but in actual fact they can see little better than humans at night but have hearing ability way in advance of both dogs and us. It was quite impossible for me to get the electric beaters ready for action without her appearing. Even if she was outside she knew what I was doing and would appear at the kitchen window. She often wandered quite a distance from the house— I wondered whether she heard me open the cupboard to reach for the beaters or picked up my thought, *'Matilda I am starting to cook.'* Whichever it was she never failed to turn up.

On one of our house moves I was embarrassed when the removers lifted a bookcase out of a corner of the lounge and revealed a large cache of Christmas Tree ornaments, a Red nose from Red nose day, and other assorted trophies; middle-aged Matilda's private store of toys.

Ironically it was the communication that flowed so freely between us that caused me such grief at the time of her death.

Matilda was an elderly but not old cat when she developed an abscess. The young vet, new to the practice insisted on anaesthetising her and lancing it. Up till then similar abscesses had always been dealt with either by me at home or if very bad by the vet giving an injection. I thought his treatment smacked of overkill. An unfortunate choice of word on my part for, down the track, it proved to be just that. I was persuaded to leave her at the surgery. She came home that night wheezy and apparently finding it difficult to breathe. I waited for her to recover from what I thought was a bad reaction to the anaesthetic; she remained wheezy. Eighteen months later she was having real difficulty breathing and had grown so weak in herself that when I heard her plea to 'Do something!' I steeled myself and called a vet who did house calls, to euthanase her. While I waited for him I sat with her telling her how much she had always meant to me.

I held her in my arms as the syringe was prepared; as the needle went into her vein she struggled with a strength she had not been capable of seconds before. At the same time I heard the words ringing in my head;

'Not this! I didn't mean this!'

It was too late. I cradled her limp body in my arms crushed by grief; in that terrible moment I felt I had failed her. I had robbed her of the chance to die peacefully without intervention, and to say her 'goodbyes' in her own time. I had thought I was doing the best for her; now I wondered, had Matilda or my own feelings been uppermost; it is not easy to watch a loved one die. Since then I have not resorted to euthanasia unless I have felt as certain as possible that really was the wish of the animal. As I made this resolve I thanked my little friend for what I thought was one last lesson. I was in for a surprise; the greatest one of all was still to come.

We buried Matilda under daffodil bulbs in a wild part of the garden; when I looked at the grave I always found myself asking again for her forgiveness.

I find it healing when a much-loved animal friend dies to write about them, often in verse, as I did for Matilda. The following I think sums up the essence of this very special cat who brought both love and laughter into our lives and imparted so much feline wisdom to me.

When Matilda reached the Pearly gates
They were surely opened wide
By angels smiling broadly
As they ushered her inside.
They would not see a plain old cat
But a bright soul truly wise
Bringing gifts of love and laughter
To the gates of Paradise.

THROUGH SPACE AND TIME

You can always talk with your beloved companion, now a friend in spirit.

Rita M. Reynolds. Blessing The Bridge

Time does not make us forget but softens grief; the year moved on and the daffodils were out when I stood by Matilda's grave remembering her, no longer with sadness and guilt but with gratitude and love for the happy years we had enjoyed. It was a beautiful Spring day, I was relaxed and in a contemplative mood when I was startled by the words in my head; for a moment I thought I really had flipped my lid, not so much because I heard Matilda but because the message seemed so crazy. *'I don't mind Marigold having my bed.'*

Two years previously I visited the local market with my six-year-old grandson. On one of the stalls we saw beautiful hand made cat igloo beds with removable synthetic sheepskin mats.

'Matilda would love one of those.' Zac, who loved her dearly, said wistfully. I agreed with him and we chose one in pale blue brocade. She loved it on sight. It was her bed, hers and no one else's for the remainder of her life; when she died I washed it carefully and stored it away in a cupboard.

Marigold was a lovely Tortie and White cat who lived with my daughter half an hour's drive away. The two cats had never met. Curiously enough it was my own sanity I doubted, not the fact that Matilda could still communicate with me from another dimension. The message itself seemed so crazy I am ashamed to say I tried not to hear it.

Less than a week later my daughter called me on the phone late at night and asked me if I would have seven-year-old Marigold to live with me permanently. She was having problems and did not wish to see her much-loved cat unhappy. I had always liked and admired Marigold so readily agreed. I remembered how she would always go and sit close to my grandson when anything upset him, the frontispiece in my book *YOUR TALKING PET,* shows her doing this, and obligingly sit in the tray at the back of his tricycle as he pedalled round the back yard.

Remembering Matilda's message I was stunned. The only spare cat bed I had available was the one that had belonged to her. I fetched it out of the cupboard and offered it Marigold; she accepted it without hesitation. For more than ten years it has been known as 'Marigold's bed'.

'By the way—I have always called her

Goldie.' My daughter told me as she got into her car to leave.

I was about to learn that cats not only know who they are but have preferences about their names. When I addressed her as Goldie she presented me with the uncompromising back view I had learned from Matilda was a rebuke. I repeated 'Goldie' in a suitably humble tone.

'My name is Marigold, call me Marigold.' The accent was on the first syllable.

I was startled into repeating it just as I heard it and was instantly rewarded when she turned round and trotted up to me with little squeaks of satisfaction.

In the years she has lived with me I have never once dared call her anything but Marigold. She responds to it wherever she is. Usually that is... my son's two little dogs had been staying with me for a week, nice little dogs who knew better than to be rude to cats. On the day he came to collect them I did not see Marigold all day. When there was no answer to my calls I became anxious, snakes were about at this time of the year. I had everybody searching for her and calling her. As the car bore the two canine visitors away she emerged from long grass only a few feet from where I was standing and where she had been sitting, watching, and listening as we all called and searched. She was quite prepared to come indoors now she had seen the visitors depart. That evening she was exceptionally loving

103

towards me; making it clear that she had very much enjoyed seeing how concerned I had been about her.

I do not consider it is anthropomorphism to credit cats with much the same feelings and emotions as we ourselves have. They are remarkably intelligent and their reputation for being cool, reserved and distant is totally undeserved. Cats are as emotional as we are—if not more so—they are capable of deep love, and also, just like us, of having their feelings hurt.

When Matilda knocked my hand and I spilt the milk I was giving her all over the floor and in doing so remembered how I had always told Tilly I would know it was her back if another cat did that, a door in my mind opened to the possibility that reincarnation was a reality, not just a nice idea. Matilda's ability to reach me from the dimension she had moved into when she left her body taught me to take note of, and more importantly act on, other messages from those who had moved on to that special place called The Summer Land.

15

FRIENDSHIPS RENEWED

*Meeting again after moments or lifetimes, is
certain for those who are friends.*

Richard Bach

As I read and thought about the doctrine of
reincarnation I began to see it as the logical
answer to many of the mysteries of life and
death. I remembered other strange cases and
stories told me about both animals and people.

'I found Tiny thrown down at the drive
gate!' I called to my husband as I drew the car
up by the vegetable garden. He stuck his fork
in the ground and came to stare at the filthy
bedraggled white cat lying in the boot .

'When I stopped to pick up the mail I
saw what I thought was a piece of paper,' I
explained, 'it was this.'

I was not surprised when he asked 'Is it
alive?'

I nodded and as if to prove it the pathetic
creature began to sneeze. Looking more
dead than alive and filthy dirty she bore little
resemblance to Tiny yet it was the image of my
beloved little friend, dead so many years ago
on the other side of the world that I saw as I

scooped her up out of the long wet grass at the side of the road.

It was early autumn and getting cool so I put her in the shed that housed the gas boiler. It was not only warm but quiet in there. She was not strong enough to cope with strange cats and dogs. I laid her carefully in a blanket lined cardboard box and managed to persuade her to lick warm milk off my finger.

By a lucky chance the vet was due that day to castrate a young donkey, I took him into the boiler house while we waited for it to come round from the anaesthetic.

'There is no way she could have walked down the Highway.' He growled, running a gentle hand over the dirty coat. She began to sneeze again and he added 'She has a bad dose of Cat 'flu, she is also just in kitten and only about nine months old.' He shook his head sadly, 'I am willing to bet she was a house pet, she must have been a very pretty kitten, then she started to sneeze, the tom cats came round, she looked like being a bit of trouble so—out.' His voice rose in disgust. He gave me tablets for her, told me to continue my good nursing and strongly advised spaying her in a couple of weeks, *if* she survived. 'She is such a helpless sort of cat.' he added sadly as we closed the door on the shed.

He was right about her being a house pet, she knew all about fridges, and what they contained, and can openers and how they opened tins of cat food, but one look at her leonine profile, so like Tiny, told me that helpless she was not. She was also blessed with the same will to live that had characterised Tiny.

We called her Sheba, She had a pure white semi-long coat, golden eyes and perfect hearing. Any one of the photos of Angora cats in late nineteenth century cat books could have been of her. Like Tiny she preferred to sleep in her own bed as close to mine as possible, rather than on my bed. I gave her a beanbag near my head. If I put out a hand in the night to reassure myself she was there she always responded with a deep purr

Her daytime resting places were varied and odd. One of her favourites was the top of the bag of dog biscuits in the pantry, she had no interest whatsoever in eating them. Outside she liked the motorbike saddle. She joined the family in the lounge in the evening and occasionally honoured me by sitting on my lap. She was the only cat I have ever known who adored chocolate. No-one could unwrap chocolate without her waking up and leaping on their chest where she made a grab, often successfully, for it before it disappeared. The easy option was to offer her a piece in the first place.

Sheba taught me healing is a two-way process. Like so many white cats she had a tendency to eczema, as she lay on my lap I was feeling through her coat and gently massaging a rough patch of skin. I had a cut on my finger that was inflamed and throbbing beneath the band-aid. When I went to bed I realised it was no longer painful. I pulled off the dressing and was astonished to find clear healed skin.

The first time she vanished I was distraught, convinced that some terrible fate had overtaken her. Three days later she was outside the kitchen window requesting admittance. Where she went and what she did we never knew, only that no one had seen a glimpse of her for three days and that she looked quite fit and well when she returned.

This happened several times over the next few years, I learned to accept her need for time out and to acknowledge that the vet had been wrong in his assessment of her as helpless. She had been away her standard three days when a horrendous thunderstorm turned the gentle creek that ran through the centre of our property to a fast flowing river. It also brought down a gum tree straight across it from one bank to the other so that it formed a natural bridge.

Through the sheets of rain outside the kitchen window I saw a white blob on the far side of the creek. Scrambling into gumboots and waterproof clothing I headed for the fallen tree calling Sheba towards it so that she could cross the swollen creek. To my horror at sight of me she plunged into the turbulent water. I stood transfixed as she swam with astonishing strength and speed against the current and climbed the bank where I stood. Her tail went up in a dripping obelisk of greeting, I could see her mouth opening but she was quite close to me before I heard her triumphant shout of joy above the storm. This was one amazing and very powerful cat.

At seven years old she was diagnosed as having a leaky heart valve.

'These...' the vet told me as he handed me the tablets he had prescribed for her, 'will enable her to live her chosen lifestyle for a while longer, then they will no longer be effective and she will go into a coma and die.' I remembered his exact words for his prognosis proved accurate.

She was dying at only eight years old, for twenty-four hours she had lain in the lounge, swimming in and out of consciousness.

'Sheba has just gone out.'

I stared at my husband, 'What do you mean?'

'She has just walked past me and out of the door into the garden.'

He sounded so convinced that I retraced my steps to the lounge where I had just seen her. She lay where I had left her.

'She can't have done.' I told him, 'she hasn't moved.'

He stared at me; then went to see for himself. His face registered disbelief and confusion as he looked down at her. 'I could have sworn she walked past me and out through the door; she was close enough to touch.' he stroked her gently; 'What did I see if I didn't see her?'

We pondered the question over coffee. Could it be that her spirit was already slipping away from her body and that was what he had seen? About six hours later she died.

I saw her again in my sleep; I had a clear dream, the sort that never seems to fade, Sheba sat in front of me; beautiful as in her prime, slowly she changed into a child in a white dress 'I have had my last incarnation as a cat,' she told me, adding with a smile before the dream faded; 'when you meet me again I shall be a child.'

Those prepared to accept the doctrine of reincarnation often have reservations about souls moving between human and animal form, what is known as the transmigration of souls. If we believe that we are souls temporarily occupying a body rather than bodies with souls and at the same time believe that animals too have souls I find no problem with the idea. Pythagoras is reputed to have said *'As wax may be stamped with various figures, melt and be waxed anew, yet always remain the same so may the same soul appear in fresh likenesses.'*

In the sixties and seventies the New Age Movement, not new at all but the resurgence of ancient beliefs, flourished, ideas and practices that have now become mainstream were eagerly embraced by those looking for a spiritual path that resonated with their own inner beliefs. Widely read at this time were the SETH books. Seth was a discarnate entity channelled by Jane Roberts, who took down his messages which were published in book form. He suggested that the soul is not a single package but can appear in different bodies at the same time. *'There is nothing to prevent a personality from investing a portion of his energy into an animal form.'* He said at one point and again, *'The consciousness that is in animals is as valid and eternal as your own …a dog is not limited to being a dog in other existences.'*

We humans, who surely are the most arrogant and self-centred of all species, like to think that the only reason cats reincarnate is to spend another lifetime with us. Love certainly plays a major part in bringing friends together again, but we are all, people and animals, here to learn and evolve

With our greater temporal power, we have an obligation to be sure that those special souls in animal bodies are able to live a life in our care that will enable them to become the best of what they are, They will do this for us— if we let them.

16

ENTER TARA

*'I had no idea that animals reincarnated …..
The animals proved it to me.'*

Amelia Kinkade

Tara's behaviour when she came into our home dispelled for ever any lingering doubts I had that animals reincarnated. Not once but many times. Tabitha Two (or Tabitha Too) I suspected had been with me before. I gave her the name the moment I saw her without pausing to consider. It suited her, she had all the first Tabitha's charm and joie de vivre. Her mother was a Tonkinese, no-one knew her paternity. She looked like a blue Burmese with darker blue tabby markings. She had the distinctive Siamese voice and she talked a great deal. I had a saddle shop in a cottage in the grounds and she loved to walk across and greet visitors with a throaty 'Hello' that sounded so much like the real thing that she earned the nickname, 'Talking Cat' from my customers . Her Tonkinese mother had led her to believe that she was far superior to other cats. I advised her on a regular basis, to be sure she looked like a Siamese when she came back so that we could all see that she was special. I was heartbroken when she disappeared. She came to me in a dream and told me she was alright but I never saw her physical body again'

A year or more later a friend told me about a young friend of hers and the Siamese stray she had adopted; it turned out to be pregnant and had just produced six kittens, five black and whites and one pure white. I had no idea then, or when the story was updated, that my beloved Tabitha was on her way back.

Each time I saw my friend she gave me another instalment. The white kitten had developed Siamese markings. By ten weeks all the black and whites had gone to new homes; only the Siamese one remained. By the time she was four months old her young owner was desperate. Her stepfather would only allow her to keep one cat. Advertisements in the local press and phone calls to all the pet shops in town had drawn no takers. The kitten's future appeared to be in jeopardy. I agreed that it was strange that no-one wanted a lovely Siamese kitten for free and did my best to dismiss it from my mind. I already had eight cats. A full compliment for any household.

'Go and look at that kitten if you want it. I have the phone number.' I gaped at my husband over my mid morning coffee. He was the rational one, I was the one carried away by sentiment and impulse—wasn't I?

'You have the number?'

'I didn't like to think of her being put down.' He admitted.

I went straight to the phone. It was Mother's Day and by the time the family gathered for a celebratory afternoon tea, an exquisite Siamese kitten was skipping round the kitchen as if she had lived there for ever.

Conversation faded as all eyes fell on the small feline figure in front of the pantry door, she studied it for a few moments; stood up on her hind legs and unerringly flicked it open exactly as Tabitha had always done, something no other cat had figured out.

We all remained silent as, after a quick appraisal of the contents, she walked across the kitchen, climbed up over the double bench to the hot plate and lifted the lid off the dog meat saucepan, again exactly as Tabitha and no other cat had done.

'That cat has come back knowing what it took Tabitha two years to learn.' My husband turned to me, 'The number of times I heard you tell Tabitha to be sure she looked like a Siamese when she came back—well—it looks as if she has.'

Quite true; with so many cats already I would never have gone out, cheque book in hand and bought a Siamese. Yet here was a kitten with no papers, no price tag and unwanted by the rest of the world even though she had every appearance of being Siamese busy establishing herself in my home and my heart.

Because I did not want anything to dent the strong bond that was there the moment we met, I took her into my shop with me the next morning and set the pattern for our life together. Just as Tabitha had loved helping in the saddle shop so Tara embraced life in a bookshop.

The job description I gave her was 'rodent controller', it was an old building and mice can be a disaster among books. They didn't stick around with Tara on the job. She also took on 'Customer Relations' ; a role she filled conscientiously and with evident pleasure gaining for herself a wide circle of friends. Like the Tabithas before her Tara loved people and enjoyed socialising.

She considered it an integral part of her job to greet people, but only if they sent out the right vibes, Whether or not she knew them, she met cat lovers by walking out into the main shop to greet them, even leaving the warmth of the gas heater in mid-winter. At times I was quite surprised, there was the tough looking driver of the delivery van who brought in a large carton of books, Tara went straight to greet him and to my astonishment he went down on his knees to talk to her. 'I love these creatures!' he told me, his face wreathed in smiles of delight at this unexpected encounter in his day's work.

At the other end of the scale there was

the woman who came in to get some photo-copying done, as she walked to the machine Tara, sitting by the heater, immediately got up and asked me to open the door so that she could go into the back part of the building. I closed the connecting door behind her and turned to my customer, well dressed and pleasant enough—I thought.

'I won't have one of those things on the place. If I see one in my garden I get someone to shoot it.' She told me as she handed me the papers she wanted copying.

One day I looked up from marking books at the counter to see Tara's hind legs and tail sticking up out of a deep shopping bag placed on the floor behind a browser.

'Tara!' I exclaimed in horror, rushing forward to remove her, the customer, deep in a book, had not noticed, she turned round now and laughed,

'Don't worry, I've got a Siamese at home—I know what they are like. There is a cooked chicken at the bottom of that bag.'

This was the first of many visits she made to the shop. Years later I met her again and we reminded each other of our enjoyable cat conversations.

One afternoon when Tara was about eighteen months old, a mother and her two small daughters came in. The younger child who was about four was almost hidden behind an enormous cardboard box. Looking slightly

116

embarrassed her mother explained that it had originally held a huge Easter egg won in a raffle, it had an oval opening in one side where the egg had been on view.

'She said Tara would like it as a bed and insisted on bringing it in for her.'

I thanked them and gave it to Tara. The child was absolutely correct, Tara did like it and slept in it until it wore out.

She was fascinated by the cash register and sat on top of it leaning over and hitting the keys. The screen with its lighted numbers intrigued her. It was very trying for the rest of us who worked in the shop for unlike a mistake we made ourselves we were never sure what keys she hit so that we could backtrack. On one occasion she clocked up a sale of $26,000 before hitting another key that caused the machine to send out a piercing wail and flash ERROR on the screen.

I learned not to leave her alone in the shop area after the night I was teaching a Tarot class in the room across the hallway when we were startled by the clatter of the cash register. The one thought in every mind, including my own, was that we had a burglar.

Fortunately it lost its appeal when my part-time assistant brought in a basket of toys for children to play with while their parents browsed. Among them were two little men, hand-made out of small pieces of wood, a face had been painted on and each wore a pointed felt hat. Tara loved these and when bored stood on her hind legs peering into the basket, rummaging among the contents with a paw till she found one which she hooked out and carried it by its hat to wherever she wanted to play. We could never find twisties when we needed one to fasten a plastic bag because Tara loved them and stole them at every opportunity.

The kitchen behind the shop had cupboards on two walls—Tara employed her cupboard opening skills here when mouse-hunting and was extremely persistent never letting up on a hunt till she had caught her prey.

At home she had complete freedom, but never hunted anything else but indoor mice. One night I had been assailed by inspiration in the early hours of the morning and was sitting up in bed writing when I was distracted by a curiously muffled yowl from Tara. She stood by my bed with a mouse in her mouth looking up at me asking if I would like it in bed. This was the first inkling I had of a mouse in the bedroom. I shot out of bed, telling her how clever she was as I explained I did NOT want it in bed. I carried her down the hall to the bathroom, in case she let it go. She almost dropped it half way but put a paw up to her mouth and held it there.

Tara was never just 'the shop cat' but a valuable staff member. If she had never done anything else her efficiency in keeping the place free of mice would have earned her keep.

She went out through the open shop door twice in all the years. I thought I had lost her for good when she disappeared the first time; in the two and a half hours she was missing I died a thousand deaths on her behalf, then I heard her unique voice and raced outside; she was running up the pavement, shouting as she came.

We had moved to a new shop the second time. Busy with a customer I did not see her leave; fortunately another customer did. He rushed to the door and out into the street calling 'Tara!—Come back!' at the top of his voice.

He looked bemused when she trotted back in and he closed the door behind her. 'Cats don't usually come when you call them like that; but I forgot she was a cat.' He shrugged at this admission, 'That's the power of her personality.'

She was still quite young, the equivalent of a human teenager, when she surprised me by her knowledge and powers of observation. One of her many friends was holding her in her arms and looking out of the window when she suddenly stiffened and began to growl quite fearsomely.

I walked to the window and followed the direction of Tara's angry blue-eyed focus. On the other side of the road the man from the next-door shop was getting into his car; it happened to be identical to mine, a red Ford Laser. Tara assumed he was taking 'our' car.

17

SHOP MANAGER

Cats are a mysterious kind of folk. There is more passing in their mind than we are aware of.

Sir Walter Scott

We had a large room behind the shop used for workshops, and meditation and discussion groups; Tara joined in them all. She also liked to sit in on visiting card readers and psychics. It was the custom to end the regular groups with coffee and biscuits. Tara, though she never asked for a drink of milk at home in the afternoon or evening, insisted on being part of this. She had her own little dish and liked milk with a dash of hot water to take the chill off it; regulars knew how to get this just right for her. The tray was always laid out on a low coffee table in the middle of the room and she never failed to check to see that her dish was there among the coffee mugs.

Ronda Pascoe, a local artist, gave me a

beautiful pastel portrait of Tara; which hung in pride of place. Ronda was also a poet, a reflexologist, and a healer. She had written booklets on healing and a volume of poetry; she asked 'Do you realise Tara is a natural healer?'

'Well, no.' I admitted.

'I have been watching her for weeks; and I have noticed that every time someone comes in and complains of a headache, a cold, or simply of feeling stressed and run off their feet, that is the person she goes and sits with and by the end of the meeting they always say how much better they feel.'

I made a point of watching her myself; and realised this was true. For several months a delightful young woman came regularly to our Course In Miracles discussion group. We all noted that Tara invariably went and sat near her. If she dropped her jacket on the floor Tara sat on it. She was a studying at the local College and when she left she came into the shop to say 'Goodbye'.

'I have learned something very important at the group;' she told me. I waited to hear the gem of spiritual wisdom she had gleaned and was most surprised when she continued, 'I shall never be afraid of cats again. I have always been terrified of them, but when Tara always came and sat near me I realised there was absolutely no need to be afraid; she is a very special soul.'

121

When David Pendragon came to read tarot Tara insisted on joining him. She settled in a deep hollow in the beanbag where she was all but invisible. I am sure most readees had no idea she was there. I asked if he minded her sitting in on sessions.

'Not a bit, I love cats. I like having her there,' he assured me. On the second day he told me of an odd experience with his last client.

'I was stressing the importance of what I was telling her; and insisting she take notice of what I was saying, for her own good. I actually repeated this several times.' He paused, remembering his exact words. 'Each time I urged her to take note and said *'Now this is important'* Tara's head bobbed up from her hollow in the beanbag and she gave her throaty yowl, I felt she was agreeing with me and helping me get the message over. It was rather weird.'

Three weeks later this person, who I had only met when she came for her reading, came back into the shop, She wagged her finger at Tara, 'I've got you on my tape.' she admonished in mock sternness before turning to me; 'It was quite creepy, each time David told me I must really take notice because what he was saying was important, she bobbed up and added her voice. It is clearly there on the tape.'

On the practical side Tara always saw things

were run as she liked. She never failed to notice when someone brought in a fresh carton of milk from the shop across the road and refused to drink the old milk. The fortnightly meeting of The Course In Miracles Group was one of her favourite days. These were held in the evening and Tara and I stayed in the shop after it closed and were joined by my friend, Rosemary, for a fish and chip tea from the shop across the road. I always bought an extra piece of fish for Tara. When we came out of the shop we could see a small figure at the glass door of the shop; as soon as she saw us she vanished, we had to go in the back way when the shop was closed, to meet us at the back door.

Another thing she enjoyed was sitting in on the Tarot classes I taught. Because she liked to interfere and rearrange my cards or those laid out by someone else, she had been banished from the room the night she scared us all by playing on the cash register. I still use a set of cards with small holes in one of them where her sharp claws punctured it as she altered the spread.

She had been sitting in on a medium doing overhead readings and it was after eleven p.m. when I opened her travelling box ready to go home. She grinned wickedly and shinned up onto the top of the highest cupboard where I could not possibly reach her. I asked her nicely to come down, I begged and entreated, and as midnight grew closer I lost patience.

'Very well,' I told her 'you can stay there the night.' I walked out and left her, knowing that she was perfectly safe.

I don't know which of us had the worst night; I suspect I did. I arrived at the shop well before opening time in the morning. As I opened the car door at the back gate I could hear horrendous wails from inside. I suspect they only started when she heard the car arrive or she would have been hoarse.

'You left me, all alone and scared,' she complained. I never again had to appeal to her to get into her box; just opened the door and she was in.

I gave up the shop when she was eight years old, and moved home three times in the remaining ten years of her life. She always walked the garden boundary and thereafter remained within it. By the time we made our last move to the twelve acre rural property where I now live she was elderly but extremely fit. In her entire life the only time she needed a vet was for inoculations. Only a few weeks before her death I walked down to the far end of it with some visitors and was amazed to find she had walked all the way with us.

A few years into her retirement I was visited by one of our mutual friends from the shop days. She asked after Tara as we strolled across the lawn.

'It's three years since I saw her, she won't

remember me.' She was saying when Tara appeared from some special hidey hole and raced across the lawn towards us shouting joyfully, she ignored me and went straight to Heather, telling her in the clearest possible Siamese how pleased she was to see her again. She stood on her hind legs and rubbed her head against her and as the final seal of affection placed a hind foot on the toe of her shoe. This was a curious little mannerism Tara reserved for her special friends.

As well as human friends she had a wonderful relationship with my dog. Ashley, intelligent and loving, was a Kelpie X Labrador. Their close friendship began when a neighbouring cat attacked Tara, in her own backyard.

I was at the window and about to rush out and rescue her when Ashley appeared and sent him back over his own fence with a great deal of noise. Tara ran up to Ashley and rubbed against her chest. I was too far away to hear but I am sure she was expressing her gratitude in her own unique way.

Ashley was terrified of thunder, Tara was not, and whenever there was a thunderstorm Tara sat close to Ashley, murmuring the soothing talk Mother cats reserve for kittens. It was most effective; Ashley was still frightened but didn't try to squeeze her portly body into impossibly small spaces or clamber on a human lap.

125

I took Ashley to the shop as well. There was a large backyard where I parked the car and she knew it was her job to guard it, and a back porch were she could sit if she wanted to come in. If there was a thunderstorm I had to let her into the back part of the shop building because she simply hurled herself in frenzy at the door. Tara always went straight to her to calm her.

Tara had rather human taste in food. Cooked chicken, fried fish, crispy chips, cooked egg, as in omelette or scrambled egg, sardines, for humans in tomato sauce, (she didn't care for those in oil or those sold for cats), and cheese. She always loved cheese.

It seemed to be a more than adequate diet, she not only thrived on it but never had a day's sickness. Even at the very end of her life she was not really ill at all, simply took to her bed by the wood stove and lapsed in and out of consciousness till she died a few days later. I missed her terribly; she had been part of my life for over eighteen years. She is buried in the garden near the house with a rosemary bush on her grave. For remembrance—but I need no reminders; Tara, a cat of immense power will live in my heart forever. Like Matilda she would also be instrumental in teaching me that communication does not end with the death of the physical body.

18

MERLIN—THE MAGICIAN

It is magic that brings an animal and a human being together in mutual understanding.

Derek Tangye—Sun On The Lintel

A flash of ginger fur vanishing under shrubs was all I saw till the evening he passed the kitchen window, thin to the point of emaciation. Nobody's cat, in a hostile world. I knew then that any home he had only existed in my imagination.

He was invisible when I placed food outside but when I let the dogs out for their last run the dish was empty.

The next night I watched from behind the kitchen window and saw him slink out from the bushes and gulp down the food before vanishing. The following night I put the food in the same place at the same time and sat silent and still in a garden chair where I could see him but not near enough to pose a threat. Just when I was about to give up and go back indoors he appeared. He gave no sign that he knew I was there, just ate and vanished.

He tested every bit of my patience and cat knowledge before he and I eventually reached not just an understanding but one of the closest relationships I have ever had with any animal.

For three weeks I watched him gulp his tea before vanishing. Each night I placed my chair and his dish of food closer. I sat very still talking to him quietly while he ate.

Eventually I was close enough to touch him; but I didn't, I merely let my hand hang at the side of my chair. It was he who made the move that sealed our friendship. He paused briefly before vanishing into the shadows and knocked his head against my hand. This was the breakthrough I had waited for and despaired of ever getting. Later that evening I watched a program on T.V. about Merlin as carer of the earth and all its creatures, the time had come to give him a name; I called him Merlin.

Each night he stayed with me a little longer. I kept up my singsong monologue interspersing his name at regular intervals and soon he was allowing me to stroke him. Our relationship moved forward in leaps and bounds now we were on touching terms and he had a name.

He was, as I suspected, an un-neutered male, so my next goal was to calm him enough to take him to the vet and have him de-sexed. Gradually I gained his confidence sufficiently for him to come inside for his evening meal and to allow me to pick him up.

I put him in a large travelling box in the middle of the lounge floor for a short time each evening after he had eaten. Here he could observe and absorb the sights and sounds of the house without feeling threatened.

At last I felt he was sufficiently calm for a visit to the vet for vaccination and de-sexing. I arranged for him to stay in overnight, as I did not want to make the fairly long trip into town twice in one day. This, as it turned out, was the best thing I could have done; what I had feared would be a traumatic experience and put him back weeks had the reverse effect.

'Oh—are you Merlin's Mum? We all love him, he's gorgeous, so friendly.'

I gaped at the girl behind the reception desk; but it was true; the caring of kind attendants during his overnight stay had finally convinced him people were nice to know. It is hard to imagine what he had endured to reduce him to such a wreck, physically and emotionally yet he could forgive.

Although I frequently get messages from animals I can never get them to reveal to me details of their past life and traumas. In that they are superior to us, they put it behind them and live in the present.

Now a handsome and powerful cat with a coat of burnished gold he was confident he had a place in the world, he was loved and loving. He stopped running from dogs; instead

129

he faced them, looked them in the eye and demanded respect. He remained reserved with strangers, particularly men, but always gave my cat-loving daughter a warm welcome when she visited and was unstinting in his affection for me. He slept on my bed and I called him my 'guard cat' when he glared out into the night and growled ferociously at any untoward noise.

I often wondered how he came to be starving on skid row for he was a brilliant mouser, keeping my feed stores and chook house free of vermin. At one time I had some donkeys living with me who belonged to my daughter; she brought large round bales of hay for them, these always housed mice. Merlin knew this and when he saw her car coming up the drive with a new bale would race to meet this fresh load of mice. He once achieved the almost impossible; I saw him on the doormat looking in through the glass door at me with what I thought was a very large mouse. I went out to thank him for the gift and saw that he had, not one, but two full-grown mice in his mouth.

After that first tentative breakthrough when he touched my hand lightly with his head he gave me so much friendship and love that I am forever in his debt.

It was my habit to walk with my dogs each morning on the golf course, crossing my own five-acre paddock to get there. Merlin was always, rain or shine, sitting in the fence

130

watching for me to return so that he could accompany me on the last lap of my walk through the garden back to the house.

I will never know where he came from; no one claimed to have lost a cat in the little village. He knew about indoor living, what litter trays were for and that refrigerators contained milk and cat food. He must once have been someone's pretty petted kitten; Life must have treated him very harshly to turn him into the traumatised outcast who turned up in my garden.

When he recovered from his initial fear of dogs he made it clear he considered them his subordinates; this was obvious when Harvey, my son's elderly Australian terrier joined the household. The first time he and Merlin came face to face was in the narrowest part of the hallway. We all three stood quite still, I was ready to rescue Merlin in case there was trouble. I needn't have worried. For what seemed a very long few minutes dog and cat stared at each other, I had the impression that a message something along the lines of *'Now get this, dog, cats rule here and I rule the cats'* was being transmitted. Not a sound passed between them, neither did either move till Harvey turned his face away and Merlin walked on past him into the lounge.

Three weeks later my son came for the weekend. 'What did you do to get Harvey to behave with the cats?' He wanted to know.

131

We were relaxing with our after dinner coffee surrounded by cats and dogs, Harvey lying across his master's lap.

'Absolutely nothing.' I answered truthfully.

'But you must have done. All his life he has been terrible with cats, nothing I did would stop him. I didn't tell you because I thought you wouldn't have him.'

'I did nothing.' I repeated, 'But Merlin did.' I described their first meeting.

Harvey lived with me for ten months before dying suddenly of a heart attack; in all that time he never treated any of my four cats with anything but politeness and respect wherever he met them. Out in the garden or inside the house. I have often thought of that initial confrontation and wondered how Merlin made it clear that ALL cats, whether indoors or out in the garden, must be respected, maybe my initial interpretation of his message to the old dog was correct.

The weight of Merlin's body on the bed, always close but not actually on top of me was reassuring, sometimes I wondered what was out there when he peered into the night and growled menacingly. He sounded so ferocious one night that I slid out of bed and switched the outside light on just in time to see a fox slinking into the shadows.

One evening he was pressed against my thigh on the couch, I was deep in a book and he stretched out a paw and touched me to get my attention. I turned and looked down into his face, as my eyes met his I was filled with a warm glow and heard the words clearly in my head; *'You don't know how much I love you— you have given me a life.'* It was a moment of sheer magic; I hope he knew how much I loved him. I had no idea then how soon we were to be parted, did he, I wonder?

It was not long after this that he went missing. I found it hard to sleep without my friend and protector on the bed. I searched, and called, and phoned neighbours. For seven years I had never slept without his comforting presence. On the second night I dreamed of him. I saw him clearly as if on film in the scrub area on my property. He had a very large rabbit and I knew that I must take it from him to prevent him eating any; I was filled with dread but I was powerless. Quite unable to make contact with him, as if we were in different dimensions or there was a glass barrier between us.

The following day I was standing at the window staring with a heavy heart at the area I had seen him in the dream, then I saw him coming slowly across the paddock towards the house. I ran outside calling his name, instead of speeding up he collapsed on the grass as if he could not take another step. As I caught him up in my arms; he leaned his head against me with a creaky purr.

Like Tilly, many years ago, he had caught

133

a poisoned rabbit, but unlike her he didn't die immediately. In fact he made a slow but steady recovery, which made it more shocking to find him dead. He was lying in one of his favourite spots under a cane lounge on the veranda. He liked it here on a hot afternoon for it afforded a dappled mixture of sun and shade. He looked so relaxed, so peaceful, so normal that it was only when the persistent shouting of my little black witch cat alerted me I realised he was dead.

I was devastated; Was it possible that the love we had shared could be snuffed out into nothing?

19

CILLA

It will be remembered that black cats are all of them witches.

Edgar Allen Poe

'I am sending you a pure black cat for luck.' My father, who had been dead for forty years, told me. The words were still in my ears and for a moment I could see him standing in front of me. Then I was fully awake. Even though I knew it was a dream with my mind, I cherished the meeting, he was just as I remembered him. As full consciousness returned I heard myself saying aloud that there was no way I could have another kitten, I had my quota of cats.

I relegated the dream to the cobwebby recesses of my mind along with the story my daughter had told me of the cat that had given birth to, and reared, a family of kittens at the bottom of a pile of tyres outside a busy workshop on a property that was a dog breeding kennels. Hardly the sort of place one would expect a mother cat to choose to raise a family.

It was not even the mother cat's home; she lived across the road and quite a little walk away. This was a wise cat who knew exactly what she was doing. Her last litter had been discovered and destroyed, no one would think of looking so far from home on someone else's property for her kittens. As she always appeared at mealtimes her people had no idea she was travelling back and forth such a distance.

I listened to the story of the discovery of five kittens already with their eyes open at the bottom of a pile of tyres with interest, because anything about cats interests me. But that was as far as it went; the cat and her kittens were back in the dim recesses of my mind when my daughter turned up at my house with a cat basket full of kittens. I had to search my memory bank when she said; 'I thought you would like to see the kitten I'm having.'

She had actually brought the whole litter to show me, they were all females but a range of colours, Tortoiseshell, Tabby, Tabby and white and her own choice, an exquisite smoky blue which she aptly called Indigo. But all I could see was a bright little black face with keen eyes peering at me over the top of the basket.

I opened my mouth to admire them; instead I found myself saying; 'If no-one is having that black one I would like her.'

I took her in my hands; 'She is Cilla; Cilla Black.' I announced after a quick inspection of the small body showed me that she was, as my father promised, pure black. No white locket at her throat, no splash of white hairs on her belly, in fact not a single white hair to be found anywhere on her small ebony person.

So Cilla came to live with me, my little witch cat, bringing with her a cornucopia of love and entertainment.

It is so unfair that dogs are given all the credit for bestowing unconditional love on their human friends while cats are considered cool and distant only offering affection in return for security and food. Many see them as lacking in emotion, other than the totally self-seeking kind, distant, reserved, even calculating. Over the years I have found this popular idea of cats totally erroneous. Cilla is proof of that. She is all emotion.

As a kitten she was wickedly mischievous

and naughty, as one would expect from a true witch cat, but this side of her personality was more than offset by her exceptionally loving nature. I was sure she brought with her not only her own love but was the bearer of my father's loving thoughts as well. She would stop suddenly in the middle of a game, leap on my lap with a trill of affection, catch my hand in one paw with claws sheathed and pull it to her face to lick it in an emotional outpouring of love. Sometimes she just looked into my face; her eyes closing in the slow blink that is the feline way of blowing a kiss.

She extended this love to my dogs, especially my Koolie, Morty, who she loved on sight. Throbbing with delight she rubbed against his chest and legs frequently washing his face for him, holding it still with her paws on either side of his jaws. He accepted this with a good grace even though at times he appeared slightly embarrassed at such an overt display of devotion.

She never showed any fear of dogs; maybe this was something to do with having heard dogs barking from the very beginning of her life and no doubt being reassured by her wise mother that there was nothing to worry about.

She has never been so brave with humans and needs to know and trust visitors before she will remain in the room with them. When a stranger enters the house Cilla disappears, only a hump under the quilt on my bed betraying her existence. From this safe hiding place she listens. At about their sixth visit she hides under the throw-over on the couch in the lounge and listens some more. Eventually when a visitor has been to the house a few more times giving her ample opportunity to listen and assess she might stay in the room with them at a safe distance, still listening carefully.

She is prepared to socialise cautiously with my close family members, but even with my daughter, who is definitely the most favoured visitor, if she feels she is outstaying her welcome she displays a fierce attachment to me, sitting on my lap and rubbing her head against me with murmurs of affection alternating with glares at the visitor that say all too clearly 'O.K—time for you to go home— Now!'

Listening is her thing. When my daughter visits and we enjoy a coffee and a gossip, Cilla sits close by in her favourite rocking chair or on the special cat stool strategically placed in the window looking down the driveway. One or other of us often remarks indulgently as her ears flick back and forth as we talk. *'She is taking in every word.'*

Leonora Faferko, a medium living in Hobart, picked up on this. She specialises in contacting animals on either side of life bringing comfort to those bereaved by the loss of a much-loved pet. I had never met her but we had been in email contact over books and our mutual interest in the spirituality of animals. I accepted her offer of a short reading for one of my animal friends, all she required was a photo and a name, so I emailed a photo of Cilla. The following is a précis of the reading she gave me.

MAGIC! 3 past lives, 2 very strong in this world. Much love from those in spirit, especially the male. (My father?) *Came to protect, teach. To give company, solace and protection. Very strong spirit energy, casts black magic away, aura cleanser. Ears hear much and eyes see much, this side and that. Has seen much in man lives. A spiritual being, greatly gifted.*

This was amazing—from someone who had never met her and knew nothing about her. I recalled the dream message from my father and smiled at the bit about her hearing much. Leonora also described her personality, how she was extremely fussy about cleanliness and very playful but at the same time there was no nonsense about her. All true.

As if to confirm the bond between us I found, one frosty winter night, as I snuggled deep between the sheets warmed inwardly and outwardly by the presence of her small furry body pressed close to mine, that my breathing perfectly synchronised with her throbbing purr. Ever since I had read the following instructions from an old Grimoire or Book of Shadows, that is a personal notebook kept by a practising witch. A sort of recipe book of spells and curses. Potions, herbs, incantations, all the information in fact that a witch, or Wise Woman would need to ply her trade I had endeavoured to do this with various cats.

Take your cat and sit together with it facing the sacred point in the sky where the moon will rise.

Run your hands gently but firmly over your friend's body transmitting love through your finger tips.

Relax completely but continue stroking until you are breathing in time with your cat's purring.

You have now become as one and you will see through his eyes and his power will be yours enhancing the power of all your spells and enchantments.

It was when I seriously tried to apply these instructions that I knew for sure that cats had a unique power; not because I achieved this union and could, indeed, see through the eyes of my guru in fur but because I found it almost impossible to do. However hard I concentrated just as soon as I was convinced I was actually breathing perfectly in time with my companion's purr the tempo would change.

Loathe to admit my own lack of expertise I came to the conclusion that the cat in question, (I tried this many times with many different cats), knew exactly what I was doing and just when to change the rhythm of its purr and thus effectively bar me from the inner

140

sanctum of its thoughts.

At last the magic had happened, I was breathing in perfect unison with my little cat's purr. True we were tucked up cosily together in bed not looking at the sacred point in the sky of moonrise but that was a mere detail and I was not going to allow it to spoil this precious moment of union with my little witch cat.

The longer I live and the more cats I know, the greater respect I have for these incredible creatures and the more aware I become of their spirituality. It is not in the least surprising that the Ancient Egyptians believed that they could lead human souls through dark labyrinths to paradise; so much of their time is spent in meditation it is easy to accept that they inhabit two worlds.

I have always believed that spirit, or soul, was not unique to the human animal and have found it possible to communicate with other living beings by direct mind to mind communication but it is the messages I have received from much loved cats who have crossed the rainbow bridge to live in another dimension that have convinced me that the life of the spirit is eternal and lives on long after the physical body no longer exists.

As an Aquarian with Gemini, another Air sign, as my Moon sign I have to accept and believe things intellectually, however much my heart tells me they are true I need to know it with my mind. I find this something of a handicap at times. For many years I have read tarot cards, even written a book about them and I devised a six week course and taught small groups. I got involved with tarot not because I was a believer but because I was a sceptic. Not to put too fine a point on it I thought, and often said, that it was a *'load of old codswallop.'* To prove myself correct I went for a reading, I was so amazed by some of the things I was told that I started reading books on Tarot and went to lots more readings with different people; my initial scepticism changed to curiosity and finally belief as I found out more of this ancient form of divination.

When Tabitha the second appeared to me in a dream and assured me she was all right I knew in my heart that her spirit still lived on but my head tried to rationalise; only the heart-breaking fact that I never saw my beloved little friend again convinced me.

When Matilda gave me the extraordinary message *I don't mind Marigold having my bed* and a short while later this was followed by a request for me to give Marigold a home both my head and my heart accepted the message had come from Matilda and therefore some part of her must still be living in some dimension. It had seemed such a bizarre comment when I received it that I had kept it to myself. I wondered about my own sanity at the time and feared that anyone else would, at best think me mad, at worst cart me off for treatment or incarceration.

One of my friends who had also been a good friend of Tara when I had my shop, confided in me one day that she would dearly love another cat herself but her husband was adamant they could not, giving as his reason that it would prevent them going away when they wished.

A few weeks later I was relaxing in a meditative frame of mind when the image of Tara, nearly three years after her death, appeared in my head, at the same time I heard an inner voice mentioning this friend by name and adding; 'she *needs* a cat, I'm working on it.' Next time I met my friend I relayed the message to her. 'Good old Tara!' was her response before adding dolefully 'she will have to work very hard.'

Another week or two passed before I heard from my friend, this time very excited, totally out of the blue a kitten was brought to her house in a cardboard box as an unexpected gift. In the few minutes that she waited for her husband to unequivocally return it whence it came this small fur person had made him her devoted slave. Probably following instructions from Tara.

It was only a month or so after this bit of successful organisation on Tara's part that once more I found her there in my head, at the same time I could hear a persistent voice telling me to go to the local RSPCA Cat shelter. It was so definite that I went to my computer and to the Shelter website. I looked through all the cats and kittens posted there but could not take my eyes from a picture of a Siamese kitten in a block of photos showing the great variety of cats and kittens that had passed through there in recent months. As I sat at the computer the message *'Go to the RSPCA'* hammered in my head. I was still staring at the screens when my daughter called in and asked me what I was doing. When I explained her response was immediate.

'We'll go in the morning. I'll come with you. I have great faith in Tara.'

Two days earlier a small group of animal lovers were in my home taking part in a workshop on communicating with animals. One of the participants was looking at a photo of Merlin. 'I can see from his photo he was a a special cat.' She looked thoughtfully at the photo then asked 'Are you thinking of getting another cat?'

'No.' I was quite definite 'nothing could replace Merlin.' He had been dead less than a year. I asked myself afterwards what or who had prompted her to ask the question.

20

MAGICAL MR MISTOFFELEES

*You ought to know Mr. Mistoffelees—
The Original Conjuring Cat!*

*T. S. Eliot.- Old Possum's Book of Practical
Cats*

'That cat has the same powerful aura as Merlin.' My daughter said as we stood in the doorway of the kitten room at the local RSPCA shelter. I stared at the kitten she was pointing out; he was a strange smoky black with white markings, in contrast to Merlin's orange and white. He was sitting on the top of a cat pedestal and staring directly at the door, almost as if he were waiting for someone; He exuded gloom and depression verging on despair. He looked directly into my face with eyes that were amber rather than yellow. My impression of our first meeting is of a room full of kittens, twenty or thirty, forming a rather blurred backdrop with this one standing out, almost as if a spotlight were trained on him. I tore my eyes away from him; he was not for me. I was looking for a dainty Siamese or Siamese Cross with blue eyes.

I did not particularly want, and certainly

did not need, another cat but the previous day the image of Tara, dead now for three years, would not leave my inner vision and neither could I silence the persistent voice telling me to go to the RSPCA shelter. I went to their website and clicked on the cats available tab, there were various cats listed then, several kittens in a variety of colours, one of them Siamese, its blue eyes looked into mine from the screen. *That's it* I thought, Tara has reincarnated and is there.

'What are you doing?' My daughter who had come to visit was standing behind me staring at the screen over my shoulder. I told her and pointed out the Siamese kitten.

'Tara has been in my head all day telling me I must go to the RSPCA.'

'If Tara says you must go, then go. I'll come with you in the morning.' Was her immediate response. By ten a.m. next day we were being shown into the kitten room. *'No—'* I was told by the attendant on duty, they had no Siamese or Siamese cross cats or kittens available at the moment. I felt I had been lured there by a false promise and mentally told Tara, that I had no intention of adopting a kitten unless I had a strong sign.

I was standing by the pedestal with the glum smoke kitten on top, almost on eye level with me. I felt a tap on my arm and turned to see one large white paw withdrawing. *If that is a sign* I thought *he has to do better than that.*

Nearly two hours later, when I had seen every kitten in the room and gone into the room where the adult cats were kept I was back again, drawn to the glum Smoke still acting 'king of the castle' on the top shelf slapping down any lesser feline who thought of taking his place. In spite of myself I was drawn to him, again he reached out a paw and touched my arm. I moved to the other side of his lofty perch, he turned round so that he was still facing me. I raised my hand to stroke him; his coat was swansdown soft; as I moved my hand away his paw reached toward me again. This time he not only touched my hand but also pulled it towards himself, still with all claws sheathed. This did grab my attention; enough for me to ask, somewhat to my own surprise,

'Is this one adopted?'

The attendant shook her head, 'No.'

She picked him up and held him in her arms.

I looked into the amber eyes and as I did so something—some knowledge of each other, flashed between us. I knew I would have him and even as I thought this his body thrummed with a rusty purr.

There was surprise, and pleasure in the attendant's eyes as she looked at me over his head.

'I always talk to him when I come in but I have never been able to get a purr out of him.' She told me as she put him down and he stalked out through the cat flap into the outside run.

Even though I knew in my heart that some sort of agreement had been reached between the cat and myself I still remained silent, running my eye over the remaining kittens, just to make sure, before turning back to the caring volunteer. Her disappointment dissolved and she smiled happily when I finally said;

'I would definitely like to adopt him.' I was still speaking when he stalked back in through the cat flap, the surliness gone, hope brightening his expression as he looked at me before jumping back on his favourite pedestal. I felt that strange jolt as something passed between us again and I knew that he had heard and understood. Feeling slightly dazed, after all I had come here convinced that I would either find my beloved Tara or zilch, but through it immensely happy, I hurried to the office to write the cheque and fill out the forms that would bind us together.

'We've called him Peanuts.' The lady dealing with the business side told me as she pushed the sheets of paper for his adoption, micro chipping and arrangements for de-sexing, inoculation and registration with the Council across the counter for me to sign; all required his name. 'Do you want to continue with it or change his name?'

'No.' I shook my head firmly, 'He is Mr

Mistoffelees.' The name came straight off my tongue without a second's thought or hesitation. Those familiar with the musical CATS or T.S. Elliott's original book will know the magical Mr Mistoffelees as the conjuring cat.

I was about to get in the car when I was compelled to look back; he was sitting just inside the netting of the outside run staring at me.

'I thought you were taking me.' He said, I sent a telepathic message winging back explaining that I would collect him from the vet in a few days time and then he would come and live with me.

It was my daughter who actually picked him up as she too had chosen, or been chosen by, a kitten so both were at the surgery at the same time. She told me that while Leroy, her kitten purred joyfully when he saw her Mistoffelees glared with a return of his old expression and made it obvious he considered she was the wrong person. That was the last time anybody has been the recipient of that glare, as soon as he saw me he smiled and became the sunny, gloriously happy cat he is today.

I was prepared for a stormy introduction to the other cats and the dogs. I had just had a friend's ten-week-old kitten staying with me throwing them all into a tizzy. But when I introduced Mr Mistoffelees there were no histrionics. He treated the dogs in exactly the

149

same firm unruffled manner that Merlin had always shown, and they greeted him as if he were an old friend returned from a holiday. The house was not at all strange to him; he knew not only the other animals but also the household routine. When I put out the dishes for cats' tea he marched into the bathroom where Merlin had always had his meals. That evening he settled on the couch by me sitting at an angle to me with his forearms resting on my thigh; this was just as Merlin so often sat. I looked down into his handsome face and smiled at the loud full throttle purr; gone was the gloom and depression, replaced by a deep happiness and glowing love; his eyes met mine and closed briefly in the slow blink of a cat kiss. I knew then that Tara had sent me to the shelter to find Merlin's returning spirit not her own and that my daughter had seen this instinctively when she said *That cat has the same powerful aura that Merlin had.'* He had been with me for a couple of days when I realised that the name that I had called him had the same meaning, Merlin was the magician, Mistoffelees the conjurer. I remembered also that I had used the words *He IS Mr Mistoffelees.'* implying that he already had the name.

He is truly magical in every way—handsome, loving, glowing with happiness. Feeling him at night on my bed, close to my side, in exactly the same spot that Merlin always chose, I thank the great goddess of all the cats that Tara was able to get through to me the need to go to the shelter and that once there the power of this incredible cat's spirit touched me.

A few months after Stoffy, my nickname for him, came to live with me something happened that shook me to the core and convinced me that I had to write this book. It was not enough for me to communicate with animals, I had to let others know how much they understood.

I was sitting in the lounge relaxing with a good book one evening, looking up I saw that Mistoffelees was sitting across the room with his eyes on me. I knew somehow that this was one of those magical moments when the lines of communication between us were sparking. I asked him why he had been so dour and glum when I first saw him at the shelter. The answer that came back was swift and to the point. *'Because they were going to kill me.'*

Even though I am well aware that far more cats and kittens go into shelters than are adopted into new homes I was startled by his reply. 'How do you know?' I asked him. *'I heard two of them talking, they said no-one wanted me so they would have to kill me.'*

Of course at that point my wretched sceptical intellectual mind took over, but I did not forget his words. Another month or two went by and I had the chance to speak on the phone to the volunteer who had been on duty

151

that day.

'Could you answer a question absolutely truthfully please?' I asked and went on to repeat Mistoffelees' words verbatim. There was a long silence on the other end of the line in which I had plenty of time to reflect she must think she was talking to a total nutter and wonder if I should terminate the call before she did.

'That is so accurate.' She finally said and went on to tell me that she had walked round with the person whose sad duty it was to decide which cats and kittens were to be euthanased in the next batch and he was marked down first of all, *'He's getting big…'* He was five months old, *'and no-one has shown the slightest interest in him.'* Was the explanation given. There was a pause and then the volunteer I was talking to added, 'If you had come two days later he would not have been here.'

I was appalled to think that he had heard and understood exactly what lay in store for him. Also how near I was to never meeting up with such a very special cat. I could understand the problem, he was getting mature and they could not keep him with the young kittens much longer, neither could they put him with the older cats without de-sexing him as there were un-neutered females among them. It is not financially viable to go to the expense of de-sexing cats on the off-chance that they will be adopted when such a large proportion never do find new homes. The policy of this particular shelter, like so many, is that when you adopt a cat you pay for de-sexing, micro-chipping, first inoculation and one year's Council registration. The cat is then sent to one of the local vets and the new owner collects it from there. This is a good system as it ensures that no cat goes out into the world without being de-sexed and micro-chipping is the greatest insurance against a cat getting lost and ending up in the shelter again.

I was told that he did not socialise with the other kittens nor make any attempt to ingratiate himself with those who came looking for a kitten to adopt. From the moment he entered my home he was a changed cat, I have never seen that sullen withdrawn look on his face, he socialises brilliantly with my own cats and also with a friend's cat who comes to stay when she is away and he is the one among my cats who almost invariably greets human visitors very politely. Ingratiation however is something he never stoops to—with anyone. I like to believe that his aloofness in the shelter was because he was waiting for me. Thanks to the insistence of my long-time friend, Tara, I did not let him down.

He is the cat with the mostest; the most handsome, the most intelligent, the most loving and the most fun; he is indeed my soul mate in fur. I feel an icy finger touch my spirit when I recall how nearly we missed meeting

153

each other.

Every now and then I catch my breath when he does something that is Merlin. I have Bantams living in large wire runs. There are some twenty metal posts and one wooden one. Merlin climbed this and spent hours sitting in one of the hen houses waiting for a mouse. No other cat has ever repeated this till Stoffy came along. He considered the wooden post briefly as if summoning memory then climbed it into the run.

He spends an hour or so out each morning while I am disposing of rubbish, getting in wood, feeding ponies and bantams and other chores. He loves to run round with me supervising and if I take too long dressing and doing indoor things before I appear, I see his face looking in at me through the window of any room I am in. Not because he wants in but because I should be out.

There is a large enclosed area at the back of the house known as the dog yard. The cats never enter it, they even get barked at if they walk past. Stoffy crosses it at will. The first time he used it for a short cut, he totally ignored the frenzied barking, simply strolled casually and even went inside one of the kennels and sat in the doorway looking out. The clear message *If I wish to walk across your yard I shall.* appears to have been received and understood; he alone of all the cats can stroll about there at will without a single canine

154

voice being raised.

I thought after a lifetime living with cats that I knew something about them, maybe understood their complex characters and what made them tick. From this extremely powerful cat I have learned that animals really DO understand what we say. When I think of the many animals everywhere who must, like him, know they are under sentence of death, I feel the least we can do is watch our words and our thoughts when we are with them.

21

THIS IS LILY

Most of us like our cats to have a streak of wickedness, I should not feel quite easy in the company of any cat that walked about the house with a saintly expression.

Beverly Nichols

My purpose in visiting Ingrid's Haven was to deliver books, adopting a kitten was the last thing in my mind. Not even when I saw three white kittens among the twenty or so playing in a Catmax Caboodle on the veranda. They looked as if they could all be from the same litter and they were noticeable for their very boisterous play as well as their white coats. White cats have always been so important in my life that I confess I was tempted; but only very briefly. I spent an enjoyable afternoon meeting the other feline residents, many of whom were walking about quite free, chatting with Ingrid and other cat lovers, and of course being entertained by the kittens. I went home quite happy that I had not succumbed to that brief moment of temptation.

It was three o'clock in the wee small hours when I woke abruptly as if the alarm had gone off or someone had shaken me awake. I had been dreaming of a white kitten; the anxious waif like face was still in my mind and a stern voice carrying over from the dream rang in my ears 'This is Lily. What are you going to do about her?'

I was wide awake, the voice still ringing in my ears and the sharp little white face still filling my mind's eye. It was so powerful it was still with me next day. I am very lucky to have a daughter whose love for cats is as great, or even greater, than my own and who has never once told me that I am imagining things. When I told her about my dream, or visitation, or whatever it was, she did not sigh and tell me I really had lost the plot this time but said she would go with me to Ingrid's to collect Lily.

When we got there I had to decide which she was. Obviously not the male for I had been given the name Lily loud and clear. I picked up one of the females and she wriggled to get down and continue her game with the other kittens and did not meet my eyes. I picked up the other one and she stared into my face with a calm unblinking gaze and I felt she was saying 'Hi—I am Lily—shall we go?'

Before I could take her Ingrid needed to take her stitches out from her de-sexing operation and micro-chip her and I had to fill in the necessary paperwork and hand over the small fee to cover the cost of de-sexing etc. When Ingrid had finished with her we popped her into the travelling box I had brought and she sat down calmly looking out while I filled out the paperwork. Her eyes were on me most of the time and I could feel her saying 'What are we waiting for? Let's go.'

She looks like a fairy cat, exquisitely pretty, but she behaves like a rough tough puppy. Although the house is littered with her toys, including a tunnel, she still considers anything not actually nailed down a potential play thing. In the six months she has lived with me she has left a trail of destruction in the form of broken ornaments etc. There was one spell when she shinned up the curtains at every opportunity, grinning wickedly from the very top where her ascent had unhooked part of the curtain from the track. Another of her favourite games is one I call 'flying cats'; in this game she tears round at incredible speed leaping from one piece of furniture to another. She has overestimated her flying skill on several occasions and crashed to the floor. On one occasion she started this game when I was in the middle of a phone conversation in an arm chair in the middle of the room and hit me squarely on the side of the head en route from sofa to table.

The magical Mr Mistoffelees is quite amazing with her, from the moment she came into the house he has loved her and she him. He plays rowdy games with her by the hour; at first I rushed to her rescue when I heard squeaks fearing he was hurting her, he is, after all at least three times her weight and size, then I discovered that the squeaks were coming not from my little fairy cat but from my great big bouncer.

He seems able to get across to her that playtime is over and calms her down with a loving wash. He not only shares his food with her but would let her take the lot if I didn't feed them their tea in separate rooms. Stoffy likes wholemeal bread or toast spread with Marmite and cut into small squares for breakfast. Lily of course muscled in on this and decided she liked it too—they clear up a large slice between them each morning, sharing a plate. Both of them love yeast tablets and take them out of the jar with their paws. Stoffy carefully and with great concentration, his aim is to transfer them from paw to mouth without dropping; he achieves this about one tablet in four. Lily has no time for such niceties, her ambition is to get as many as possible, as quickly as possible, so she scoops several out at once.

Of course she is not all terrible tiger cat; She is proud of her beautiful white coat, soft silky and semi long with an elegant plume of a tail. With Stoffy's help she moves in a sparkling white cloud and smiles with pleasure when visitors remark, as they always do, on her beauty. She is obliging and philosophical about going into her special bedchamber, a large dog carrying crate, at night and doesn't even demand to be let out in the morning. I stuck a little sticker on it I purchased at a Mind, Body, Spirit Festival; it bears the legend *Goddess In Training*. There are times when I feel she has a long way to go, others when I know without doubt she will make it.

My grandchildren love her because she is always ready to play, the wilder and rougher the better. She is the only cat I have ever known who puts so much into a game that she ends up panting. When this happens I call a halt and make her rest.

This is Lily, loving and lovable, exquisitely beautiful, brave and sensible yet totally zany. She is a source of great joy filling my world with love and laughter.

If I were asked to sum up her personality I would say it is her zest for living, her enjoyment of the life God gave her. What a wonderful world it would be if we were all like her.

My journey through life has always been in the company of animals. Cats have always been there, travelling alongside me, I owe them so much, they have given me so much companionship, affection, even a reason to keep going in the bad patches.

I view each life as a learning experience, a chance to grow spiritually; in this life the wonderful animals I have known of many different species, have taught me so much about courage, love and forgiveness that I can no longer accept the superiority of human beings and our right to treat them as things to use and dispose of as we choose. Lily, with her abundant joy in just living has made me feel that there has to be a better way to control the cat and dog population than killing.

Visiting Ingrid's Haven and seeing the difference one person can make to so many lives and experiencing the atmosphere among the cats who know they are safe in contrast to those in conventional 'shelters', many of whom, like Mr Mistoffelees, must be well aware they are not, has been a wake-up call for me. Ingrid is a true cat lover who was appalled at the number of cats and kittens killed each year because no one comes forward to offer them a home. Many of us are equally appalled but it takes someone like Ingrid to do something about it. She started a cat sanctuary worthy of the name which she called Ingrid's

Haven. Any cat or kitten that ends up there either stays for the rest of its life or is adopted out to a good home. We can not all open shelters but we can raise our voices to protest about the selling of puppies and kittens in pet shops. This alone would help to stamp out the puppy mills that supply them.

Most young children know instinctively what their animal friends are feeling and thinking but a 'rational' world can obliterate this knowledge. Adults who tell children they are imagining the messages they get from animals do both a great disservice. The secret of successful and meaningful communication lies in the ability to become again as a little child and to allow one's inner self to contact the inner being of the animal. This means relaxing, listening to the voice within and trusting what one hears.

I have learned over the years that animals are really just like us, there is far more to them than the outer physical form we are familiar with; if we are a soul with a body, rather than a body with a soul then so are they.

I have enjoyed my walk down memory lane with just some of the cats who shared my journey; I hope you have too. These wonderful cats enriched my life, they exemplified the power inherent in all cats, yours as well as mine. I hope reading about them enhances your appreciation of those who share your life and deepens the bond between you. There are few experiences more enriching than the human animal relationship when it is based on mutual love and respect. Anatole France recognised this when he wrote; *Until one has loved an animal a part of one's soul remains unawakened.*

BOOKS TO ENJOY

KINDRED SPIRITS by Allen M. Schoen D.V.M., M.S. A book by a holistic veterinarian about the spiritual bond between animals and people. Random House. First published 2001

JAMES HERRIOT'S CAT STORIES. St. Martin's Press. 1994

THE NINE EMOTIONAL LIVES OF CATS. A Journey Into The Feline Heart. By Jeffrey Masson. Random House First published 2002

THE CAT WHO CAME FOR CHRISTMAS. The Story Of Polar Bear. By Cleveland Amory. Bantam. First published 1988

ASK YOUR ANIMAL. Resolving Behavioural Issues Through Intuitive Communication. By Marta Williams. New World. 2008

KINSHIP WITH ALL LIFE. By J. Allen Boone first published by Harper and Row in 1954.
This book has become something of a classic on animal communication.

REDEMPTION. by Nathan J. Winograd. Almaden Books 2007. the myth of pet overpopulation and the No Kill revolution in America. This book, which is basically the history of the move towards a more enlightened and humane approach to the problem of unwanted pets is not something to flick through in a spare half hour but is a very worthwhile read and a valuable reference for anyone concerned for the welfare of domestic cats and dogs. This book has won five major awards and was re-printed in 2009 with extra material.

CATS IN THE BELFRY by Doreen Tovey This was the first of a series of books by author Doreen Tovey on life with Siamese cats. It was followed by CATS IN MAY and is probably one of the most popular cat books ever written. These two were first published in the 1950s by Eleck books.

www.annwalkerbooks.com to see my other other animal books, tapes and CDs. Have your say on the Blog and find Links to other sites about animals.